A.I.M.

A.I.M.

The Powerful
10-Step
Personal and Career
Success Program

Jim Carlisle and Alex Gill

John Wiley & Sons Canada, Ltd.

Library and Archives Canada Cataloguing in Publication Data

Carlisle, Jim
 A.I.M. : the powerful 10-step personal and career success program / Jim Carlisle, Alex Gill.

Includes index.
ISBN 978-0-470-73760-6

 1. Self-actualization (Psychology). 2. Career development.
3. Success. I. Gill, Alex II. Title.

BF637.S8C367 2009   158.1   C2009-906126-0

Production Credits
Cover design: Joanna Vieira
Interior design: Mike Chan
Typesetting: Thomson Digital
Cover image: istockphoto.com
Printer: Friesens

John Wiley & Sons Canada, Ltd.
6045 Freemont Blvd.
Mississauga, Ontario
L5R 4J3

Printed in Canada

1 2 3 4 5 FP 14 13 12 11 10

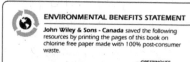

ENVIRONMENTAL BENEFITS STATEMENT

John Wiley & Sons - Canada saved the following resources by printing the pages of this book on chlorine free paper made with 100% post-consumer waste.

TREES	WATER	SOLID WASTE	GREENHOUSE GASES
42	19,181	1,165	3,983
FULLY GROWN	GALLONS	POUNDS	POUNDS

Calculations based on research by Environmental Defense and the Paper Task Force.
Manufactured at Friesens Corporation

Table of Contents

Part III: Wrapping Up and Looking Forward

Acknowledgments

Jim and Alex would like to thank their respective spouses, Lynne and Karen, for their support, encouragement and patience.

Jim offers a special thank you to all of his clients whose trust, experiences and feedback have made this method possible.

Alex would also like to thank his family, especially his sister Sandra, whose sun porch overlooking the Bay of Exploits served as a writing studio for many of the chapters in this book. He owes a debt of gratitude to Robin Chetwynd, the visionary CEO whose belief in coaching allowed Alex to first work with Jim Carlisle, a journey that ended many years later with the publication of this book.

How Coaching Changed My Life—and Can Change Yours

by Alex Gill

Ten years ago, I was living two lives.

My outward life, the one my family, friends, and colleagues saw every day, seemed to be going pretty well.

I had been out of graduate school for only four years but was already the communications director for a large and respected non-profit. The team I led was made up of smart, committed people who were a joy to work with. I managed a sizeable budget and was able to do very creative things as part of my work. We created advertising, awards shows, and glitzy events. We implemented some of the first e-commerce websites in the nonprofit sector. We changed how the organization marketed itself and how it listened to its supporters. I was one of the organization's media spokespersons and regularly appeared in newspapers, on the radio, and on TV. To top it off, I had just gotten married and was looking forward to building my professional and personal life.

To an outside observer, this was the latest chapter in an upbeat story. A person from a modest background gets a good education and rises quickly to a senior position, with many more steps yet to climb. Recruiters were already calling to talk with me about new, more senior jobs at other organizations. The sky—it seemed—was the limit.

There was only one problem.

In my inner life, that few people saw, I was deeply unhappy.

At the end of the workday, I would linger in my corner office over a pile of paper that never seemed to get smaller. The work I was accomplishing gave me less and less satisfaction. When I came home, I would talk with my wife about the problems at my workplace—friction with the board, volunteers, other employees, and competing organizations. Whenever I talked about what I did, all I seemed able to do was complain.

I was turning into someone I did not recognize or respect. When I stepped back and listened to myself, I heard a person who was whining about what was happening to him, but who did not have a strategy to address the very things that bothered him. Looking at myself from the outside, I was beginning to hate who I saw. I was the type of person who should know what to do, who had always had a path and a purpose, but I now lacked the courage, conviction, or knowledge to make a change. What changes could I make? Did I have what it took? Could I afford to take the risk—to do something that might cost me the position, the salary, and the status that many other people seemed to want and value? Other people seemed quite content with the type of job that I was having trouble enjoying—what the devil was wrong with me?

I was stuck in a rut and I couldn't see a way out. Then, I met Jim Carlisle, and he became my executive coach.

Jim Carlisle was part of an overall change we were trying to achieve at my organization. One of my responsibilities had been to set up and oversee an organizational change process. The change team I established considered several ways to improve the organization's operations. At the top of its list was to bring in an executive coaching program for the CEO and the department heads, such as myself. So, in 1999, just at the time when I was secretly despairing about my life and what I could do in the future, I chose Jim to be my coach.

If the truth be told, I didn't really think that coaching would make that much of a difference in my life. I thought I would learn a few new things. Perhaps I would improve my management skills. Maybe Jim could tell me how to be a CEO one day. When we first met, I remember that my expectations were not exactly high.

When I first saw him, Jim struck me as a likeable, affable guy. Tall with graying hair and glasses, he looked a little like what you would expect a casting director to send you if you said, "I need a CEO in his mid-fifties." Unlike many of the CEOs I had met, however, Jim was different. Instead of a "take-no-prisoners" approach that involved competition and command from the start, Jim simultaneously managed to convey openness and discipline. You knew he was serious about what he was doing, but he was open to talking with you about what was on your mind.

Settling into the guest chair opposite my desk, Jim spread his hands expansively and said, "Well, tell me about yourself."

I started by describing my current job, going on to give him the standard biography I would have recited to any business colleague. My modest family origins, the universities I had attended on scholarships, and the jobs I had held. Then I returned to my current job, beginning to catalogue all that I thought was wrong with the organization and what I had to do to fix it. It was, I thought, a pretty compelling story that anyone would want to hear and would be able to understand.

Jim stopped me in mid sentence with a smile and a friendly wave.

"No, no, no . . . we'll get to all that," he said. "But first, tell me: What is it you *really* want to do?"

I was a little taken aback by that question. Wasn't he listening to me? Hadn't I just told him about what my organization needed, about my quick rise to my current position? Wasn't this exercise just supposed to give me some new tools and skills to be a better executive? Perhaps he had not understood me?

But as we talked more, it became clear that Jim understood me all too well. With his practiced eye, he had seen through the story I had put up like some Potemkin village. By the end of that first conversation, I admitted to Jim that I wasn't really sure if I had ended up in the right place, or if the direction in which I was going so quickly was a direction I thought would make me happy.

In the days and months that followed, Jim had me work through a number of exercises that we will share with you in the pages of this book. I summed up my life story, decade by decade, highlighting those things that I thought had brought me to where I was. We addressed my work challenges, putting them in an entirely new perspective that made me more effective. I began to map out some directions to explore further, meeting with others both inside and outside my field to talk about their lives and their work.

When I met others and talked with them, a new world slowly began to open up. I started to see my current job as just that— my current job. The struggles I was going through, the things I worried about that denied me sleep at 3 a.m., were just part of the most recent chapter of a book that was not yet complete. In the stories I heard from other professionals, I began to see limitless opportunities that I had not even begun to think about. There were very challenging and interesting fields that I had never heard of, places and issues that allowed people to grow and prosper, but most importantly, they could do so in a manner and at a pace determined by them.

When this realization sank in, things began to go much more smoothly at my job. I found new ways to approach issues that had stymied me for weeks. I became a more productive member of my management team, bringing some of the new perspectives that I was learning outside the organization to bear on issues on the inside. At home, I relaxed more and stopped complaining so much about work. I also started to sleep through the night, as the worries that had kept me staring at the ceiling didn't seem so pressing anymore.

As Jim and I worked through my path, we met in the wood-paneled library at his condo building. Over coffee, I would tell him all that I was learning about my job and myself. Jim, in turn, asked probing questions that helped me to better understand this information and use the new perspective I was gaining to climb out of the rut in which I had found myself. Through months of work, I went from someone who was skeptical about what a management coach could do, to an enthusiastic convert who was ready to address any challenge and overcome it.

This new mindset could not have come at a better time. As anyone who has worked in a changing environment knows, just because you feel you are on the right path does not mean that the world will organize itself around you. The world can change on a dime, and this happened to me when a new board fired my CEO and suspended the work of my change team. As the chief champion of change, I found myself at the receiving end of a polite conversation about what it would take for me to move on to another employer.

Had this happened a year previously, I would have been devastated by the rejection of an organization to which I had committed so much time and energy. The potential loss of my position, with its accompanying status and salary, would have knocked me for a loop. While I was surprised and disappointed, the work I had been doing with Jim in the months up to that point now paid enormous dividends. In the comfortable confines of Jim's library, I remember calmly facing him over the coffee table and saying, "I'm ready to move on, I'm going to make this work for my benefit."

A few weeks later, with a severance package in hand, I began contacting those people I had met through my outreach to discuss where "neat" things were happening. Where could someone with my skill set and appetite for change begin to make a difference? These contacts quickly led me to a senior position at another challenging organization, where I helped build a $5 million nonprofit from the ground up. Two years later, after another unexpected CEO departure, I found myself, at the age of thirty-three, stepping into his position to help the organization survive a time of turmoil. In the positions that followed, I grew as a person and never stopped putting the principles of A.I.M. into action.

Today, I run my own firm, which helps dozens of nonprofits improve their community impact each year. I work on very interesting and socially relevant projects for an ever-growing roster of clients. I have flown around the world to talk about community building, environmentalism, and social marketing. I also teach at an innovative downtown university where the students are a joy to teach and my fellow professors often remark on my enthusiasm for my work and life in general. My friends and family constantly note that I seem happier and more motivated as the years go by.

This did not happen because of some exceptional piece of luck or some superhuman ability or intelligence on my part. Far from it. I was not an exceptional person who was one out of ten million. I was someone who happened upon a method—the A.I.M. method—that helped me to determine who I was, what I would be happy doing, and then put me on the path to achieving it. It happened because I put those principles into action with the help and guidance of a coach like Jim Carlisle.

Before A.I.M., I was just an ordinary guy with a problem that many, many others have had at some point in their careers. I was unhappy. I was becoming bitter. I complained about my job a lot. I knew I was in a rut and couldn't figure out what to do about it. I felt powerless, unfocused, and alone. And I wasn't able to see a way I could make things improve.

That was my starting point before I began the A.I.M. process. And the end result speaks for itself, just as it speaks for the experiences of the dozens of other people you will meet in this book. Their experiences—much like mine—show that my situation is a fairly common one and also that, given the right method and encouragement, ordinary people can achieve great things.

After Jim and I ended our coaching relationship, we continued to stay in touch. Meeting over breakfast every few months, he and I would share our concerns about life. We grew to be friends and, as we did, I began to tease him about sharing his approach.

"Jim," I would say every time we met, "when are you going to write a book? There are millions of people who are where I was. They are unhappy and they need a way out. You should really share the A.I.M. method with them."

Jim brushed off my comments for years until one day, totally unexpectedly, he mischievously replied, "Okay. I'll write a book if you will write it with me."

What could I do but say yes? That exchange, over a coffee and breakfast, began a journey that ended with the publication of this book.

With that slice of my story, I hope readers can appreciate how A.I.M. changed my life—and how it could help you to change yours. Despite having busy and productive lives, Jim and I have taken the better part of a year to write this book because we believe strongly in helping those who need a way out. Every day we see people who would benefit from taking charge of their lives and moving forward to achieve, inspire, and make a difference.

If you see a bit of yourself in my story—or in the dozens of stories we will share in this book—read on. I hope your journey will be even more productive and rewarding than my own.

Enjoy the book!

What Is the A.I.M. Method All About?

Only I can change my life. No one can do it for me.

—Carol Burnett

Welcome to the A.I.M. method. You have joined my co-author Alex and I on a journey where, if you are willing, we will take you through a series of steps that can change your life.

That is a bold statement with which to start a book—but here are some bolder ones.

You have chosen this book because, while you may not have realized it, you are playing a part in two very troubling issues. First, you are one of millions of people around the world who, to some degree, feel stuck, unmotivated, trapped, overwhelmed, and unhappy. This silent army doesn't show up in opinion polls or demonstrate in public squares—but they are out there, staring at their ceilings in the middle of the night, running through their lives in their minds, and wondering why they can't sleep. They often lack the words or direction or context to do something about it, blaming themselves, their workplaces, their families, and others around them because they just can't get it right. The many reasons people feel this way are not immediately clear to them. They don't see that workplaces have eliminated entire ranks of managers who once used to mentor and counsel their employees. They don't see that life has become so busy that it has diminished the role that friends and family used to play in helping them think through their challenges. They don't see that a busier society that increasingly relies on electronic communication doesn't create the natural time and space for self-reflection and honest talk about the important things. In short, they don't see that everyone is in the same boat. They believe it is just their problem and, consequently, bear the weight silently and alone.

These people have vague, unfocused thoughts—perhaps as you do—that they should be doing something differently, something that would make them happier and more fulfilled. However, if you asked them what that "something" was, they lack the words to tell you. They might talk in generalities about a new job, a new relationship, moving to a new city, starting a new sport, or some other incremental change that they think might make them happier. They may even have tried to make those changes in the past, only to end up basically where they started—still unhappy and wondering why.

The second issue is an extension of the first one—and is even more troubling. If you are unhappy as an individual, and there are millions of people like you around the world, what does that mean for any impact you might make over the course of your life? If millions of people feel stuck and alone and do not think they are reaching their true potential—what impact does all of this unhappiness have if we add it all up? What example can legions of unhappy people offer to their family, their friends, their colleagues? What changes can they truly make in their workplaces or communities? What difference will they make with respect to the major challenges that face us all? The answer, unfortunately, is that they will probably not make a difference. They will either accept their unhappiness or only make small changes throughout the course of their lives when they could have taken steps to effect true change in their lives. They will find themselves in jobs or personal situations that are "just okay," ones that do not challenge them to move forward, to become happier, and to become an example to others.

Now, imagine for a moment what the situation could be like if it was reversed. What would happen if we could help people identify why they were in their current, unfulfilled situations and then figure out what might make them happy? Imagine if we helped them identify options that could change their lives and supplied them with the concrete steps and tools they need to move in a positive direction. Imagine if, one by one, they found ways to feel more in control of their lives, more engaged in their jobs and personal lives, and, as a result, became happier overall. Imagine if, when they became happier people, they focused on helping others around them, giving back to their families, friends, and communities. What begins as a small change for individuals could become a bigger change that affects us all.

That is what the A.I.M. method is meant to do—to help people, as individuals, start on the path towards realizing their true potential. By doing this, it can help more people to care, more people to engage, more people to make a difference for themselves and everyone around them.

A.I.M.: Achieve, inspire, make a difference

The A.I.M. method, as the name indicates, has three parts. The "A" stands for "achieve" and answers that deep-seated need we all have for a sense of achievement in our lives, a sense that we have somehow faced an obstacle and overcome it. This feeling of accomplishment is not confined exclusively to a professional or career achievement, although the method is well suited to allow you to do that. Achievement can come in many forms—personal goals, milestones you never thought you might reach, or accomplishing something beyond your perception of your own abilities.

The first and most important steps of the A.I.M. method help you identify your challenges and move towards achieving them. But once that process is underway, you begin to move towards the other two portions of the method that are just as important. The "inspire" segment begins as you realize a sense of all the possibilities that you might take advantage of, through the research you conduct and networking with others. At some point, you will begin to gradually shift from someone who requires the help of others, to someone who, through your example, inspires others to begin the same journey. As you progress further along that path, as your network becomes fully developed and you begin to move in directions you never believed were possible, you will reach the final portion of the A.I.M. method where you begin to "make a difference." Engaged in your life and in control of your own destiny, you are not only inspiring others through your example, but also are in a position to actively give back to those around you. People who are "turned on" to their own possibility, who can make things happen with respect to their own life, are often at the center of helping and inspiring others to make a difference in their lives. That is the final and ultimate stage of the A.I.M. method.

This end point may seem like a lofty goal that is a long way away from where you see yourself now. While there are no shortcuts, A.I.M. offers a proven process, laid out in manageable pieces that anyone can complete, which will start you moving through those three phases towards that long-term goal.

Through these three main parts, the A.I.M. method is a practical, 10-stage program that will help you turn your vague desire for change into a reality. It begins by helping you first look within, leading you through a few self-analysis exercises that identify the issue you will focus on, followed by an exploration of what you value, what has happened to you throughout your life, and an examination of your strengths and weaknesses. Armed with this information, we will then identify some possible options that may be a fit with your new understanding and, through a series of exercises, narrow these options down to a manageable number. Having identified your best options, we will then lead you through a process of research and strategic networking to explore them more fully, uncovering additional areas and new contacts that can broaden your understanding and make you a more resilient person. Finally, we will move from focusing on what benefits you, to what can benefit others, using your progress through the A.I.M. process as an example to people around you.

Ten Steps of the A.I.M. Method

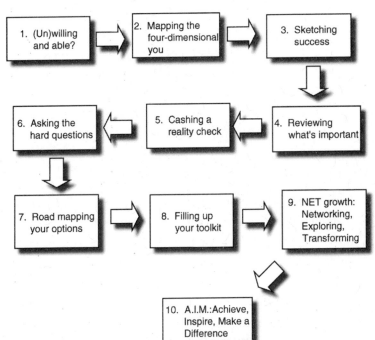

This process has been followed by hundreds of CEOs and top executives. While it may seem straightforward, it is not. It is based on the following key interrelated principles:

1. **Focus makes direction possible.** No matter at what stage you find yourself in your career or life, if you can identify a manageable challenge and articulate what you have to do in order to address it, you are definitely ahead of the curve. Conversely, my experience with coaching clients has shown that people who cannot identify, with clarity, what they are trying to do are the ones who struggle, who are often stuck and more likely to feel helpless. A huge challenge is often insurmountable, but a definite objective you can do something about can put you on the road to change. This is why A.I.M. has, as one of its first stages, the identification of what you are trying to address through the process.

2. **There is more to your life than your career.** This is an often-repeated truism, which would not be necessary to repeat so often if people actually took it to heart. Of the many facets of our lives, the one that most clients want to talk about is their career. Yet we all have many intriguing aspects of our lives that affect who we are and how happy we can become—and the people who understand that are the most likely to succeed in following the process. This is why A.I.M. focuses on the four dimensions of personality, not exclusively upon a person's career success.

3. **Knowing where you came from helps you go somewhere.** It is important to know what you have done in the past, why you have done it, and how those actions fit in the overall narrative of your life. My clients who did not understand this were often doomed to make the same mistakes, respond in the same way to the same types of challenges, and end up in a similar position to where they began. This is why A.I.M. contains exercises that help you review your history, identifying any recurring patterns and ensuring that you are aware of your strengths and weaknesses.

4. **Knowing yourself gives you a base to move outwards.** I have found that the clients I have coached who understand the previous principles and are able to take stock of their lives in a logical and objective manner, are the ones who are most likely to brainstorm valid options for moving their careers or lives forward. For this reason, A.I.M. insists that you conduct a number of self-assessment exercises before you move on to the later stages.

5. **Others are essential to validating your assumptions.** It is fairly easy for people to get wrapped up in their own self-analysis that may, or may not, be all that accurate. Those clients who were able to honestly check in with others who knew them to present their self-analysis and ask, "Does this sound like me?" were the ones who were most likely to successfully complete the process. This is why A.I.M. contains a number

of stages that ensure that others outside of your process can weigh in on your assumptions.

6. **Honesty about capacity prevents disappointment.** It is fairly easy to identify a number of options you could explore, and we often rush to do so without thinking about the time, our commitments, or other factors that can influence whether we are able to really explore them properly. Of my clients, those who knew their limits were the ones who could narrow their focus to what really mattered and make manageable progress. A.I.M. contains a series of steps that force you to ask hard questions about whether you are capable of making change happen for this very reason.

7. **Preparation before action.** The A.I.M. method encourages you to conduct extensive research on the options you identify and helps you to create a number of "tools" that will help make your journey easier through the latter stages of the process. Human beings often want to act instead of prepare, but experience has proven that clients who take the time to think through and write down, for example, what they are going to say to a possible networking contact are the ones who are most likely to improve their odds of success. That is why the "action" part of A.I.M. comes so late in the overall method, and why people have to complete the initial stages in order to maximize their possibility of success.

8. **Networking is more than meeting people.** I am continually surprised by how misinformed people are about networking. While most coaches will tell their clients networking is important, their understanding of what it is and how to do it properly is often superficial and limited to the basic advice of "get out and meet people." Unless you are very gifted in this area, the results are usually disastrous. The success of the latter stages of A.I.M. rest on strategic networking that will connect you with an ever-expanding group of contacts that can help you explore and realize your options.

9. **The end is the beginning.** Once clients have begun to attain the initial goal they outlined at the start of the process, many of them incorrectly see the A.I.M. method as complete. However, attaining your original goal is only the start. The true realization of A.I.M. comes when you make it part of your everyday personal and professional life, meeting others to build your support network, and actively giving back to those around you.

From the C-suite to you: The origins and history of A.I.M.

A.I.M. is grounded in a simple approach: What if we took the coaching method used by more than 500 top CEOs and up-and-coming executives to address their challenges and made it available to everyone?

In order to appreciate the value of this approach, let us first explain the profession of coaching and the origins of the method itself. While "executive coaching" is a relatively new discipline, it has always been with us in some form or another. The earliest kings and nobles had advisors at their courts that could offer them an informed perspective on the decisions necessary to govern. In aboriginal cultures, one of the vital roles that elders played was to serve as a source of perspective, traditional knowledge, and advice on important decisions. Even organized crime families made famous in Hollywood movies had their *consigliore* to provide the Don with advice and counsel that was at arm's length from the family hierarchy.

The modern economy introduced a new aspect to this situation. As industries grew and became increasingly complex, the concept of "management" became correspondingly complex. And one of the expectations that managers took on was the responsibility for their employees' well-being. Not only were managers supposed to encourage greater productivity as the workforce shifted away from the shop floor and became increasingly service (and office) based, but they were also expected to mentor and advise their employees, helping them develop and make a better contribution.

That expectation survived, more or less, until we began to re-think traditional models of corporate hierarchies in the 1970s. No longer were managers a given part of the structure—they increasingly became an endangered species as successive waves of restructuring redefined and flattened the corporation. Whether we called it "re-engineering," "right-sizing," or another of a succession of popular terms, the result was the same. In a relatively short amount of time, we eliminated entire ranks of middle management and asked those remaining to take on more responsibility, work harder, and focus more on productivity.

While these new approaches resulted in leaner, more competitive organizations, something very important was left out of the mix. Managers across the modern corporation no longer had the time to quietly mentor their employees, talk with them, get to know them as people, and, over time, help them realize their career and personal goals. Employees were expected to absorb generations of knowledge either through osmosis or by taking occasional seminars or training sessions that they squeezed into their already demanding schedules.

Added to this time squeeze was the fact that corporations were no longer offering "jobs for life" to their employees. Employees at every level were now expected to move many times, often spending just a few years with any one employer. This decrease in tenure made it far less likely that any employee would develop the internal relationships necessary to learn the important lessons of corporate culture.

And this time crunch and lack of tenure extended all the way to the top of the corporation. Where CEOs and executives had once commiserated socially with their peers inside and outside the corporation and taken their time to learn their craft, the pace and expectations of the modern corporation allowed little time for such unstructured learning or informal mentoring. CEOs and executives became just as interchangeable as their employees and spent more and more of their time focusing on boosting quarterly results and increasing productivity at all costs. As one CEO remarked to me in the 1980s, "It's produce or die these days, and you don't want to end up on the wrong side of that."

By the 1990s, companies were facing serious challenges. How to develop the next generation of executive leaders, when the current generation was too busy, too distracted, or too scared to talk with them? How could executives make the best decisions and contribute more to their organizations if there was no place for them to go for advice and help?

From this need, the idea of the external "executive coach" was born. If the corporate structure needed—but could not provide—the perspective and advice to help its employees and inform its senior decision makers, then they would outsource this function. This is why the 1990s saw the emergence of a new type of professional—the executive coach. Drawn from the experienced ranks of current and former executives, consultants, and other professionals, these coaches are equipped with the life and work experience necessary to provide the perspective that is lacking. And as consultants operating independently of the corporate structure, they also fit within the models of outsourcing that have sprung up as corporations shift non-core operations outside the corporation and access them on a fee-for-service basis. Executive coaches have evolved to a point where top executives now rely on coaching to improve their performance, just as top athletes rely on coaches to keep them at the top of their game.

While there are a lot of different ways to approach executive coaching, for me, a typical client relationship might evolve in the following way. Through a referral, a request, or a selection process, I would meet with a CEO or senior executive who was facing a challenge. In some cases, the challenge may be purely in the realm of the workplace: high performers who may be lagging and their superiors may want to help them; CEOs who may be going through a time of incredible change or stress and need someone outside the firm to talk with about the choices they have to make; or young up-and-comers in a company who may have exhibited some of the qualities that attract the attention of upper management, and they decide to offer them some personal development help.

In other cases, the driver to seek coaching advice may be largely personal: senior professionals who, while successful, may be experiencing a crisis of confidence and wonder whether they have made the right choices; executives who may have experienced repeated personal or professional setbacks and may want to work through options about where they can best apply their talents to make a difference; or executives who may have been unexpectedly terminated from their jobs and need help considering their lives beyond their former positions—or whether it is time for a life change.

In all of these cases, executive coaching has value, because it delivers something the most highly trained professional, the most senior executive, or the most self-reliant strategist cannot necessarily do themselves. And that "something" is an external perspective on their challenges, backed by experience and a professional framework that only an executive coach can provide.

You would think that when someone becomes a CEO or senior executive that they would be so well qualified, with such well-honed skills and strengths, that they would be able to tackle any problem or challenge successfully. Fortune 500 CEOs, you might believe, are highly qualified and motivated to get to the top—what help could they possibly need once they are at the top of their game?

I've heard these comments so many times. They rest on the assumption that successful people are somehow fundamentally different than you and me. There is one major problem with this assumption—it's completely wrong. From my decades of work with senior business leaders, I can say that most of them are pretty much like you and me. Sure, they may be more successful, make more money, and have more responsibilities than most of us, but when you drill down to talk with them one-on-one, what you find isn't surprising—they're very human. They have their own anxieties, their own self-doubts. They have limitations and worries that keep them up at night, and they have their blind spots which are keeping them from realizing their full potential. This is where executive coaching comes in. No matter how successful an executive is—he or she can always benefit from an external perspective and a logical process to help them identify problems and act on them.

But what impact can talking to someone and doing some self-evaluation exercises really have? Can executive coaching truly make a difference in an individual's life or in the life of a huge corporation?

Without a hint of exaggeration, I can say that I have witnessed people completely change their lives after a period of successful executive coaching. I have seen CEOs accelerate from bland caretakers to dynamic leaders, taking their companies in whole new—and profitable—directions. I have watched as executives who were in danger of stalling at a midpoint in their careers moved on to positions of true leadership, developing capabilities that they and their companies assumed they did not have. And I have seen others take a different (but no less rewarding) path, leaving a burgeoning and lucrative business career and embracing a new direction that has led them to live a much more fulfilled and open life.

In making these dramatic changes, these executives were each beginning a journey similar to the one I began more than thirty years ago. At that time, there was no A.I.M. method; "executive coaching" didn't exist yet.

Starting on the road to A.I.M.: My experience

In the preface to this book, my co-author Alex shared his introduction to the A.I.M. method. He talked about not knowing why he was unhappy, but after meeting me and adopting my method, he was able to work his way towards independence and success. My own journey began before coaching had taken hold in the corporate world. What I learned through my attempts to deal with my own unhappiness led, many years later, to the stages that would become A.I.M. It all started when I gathered up enough courage to walk into my then-boss's office in the early 1970s to answer a basic, but very dangerous, question.

I can still remember that late spring day. It was an office exactly like those occupied by other executives at the bank in which I worked at that time. There was some basic furniture, file trays, family pictures, an unremarkable view of a downtown street, and Walter—my boss—sitting across from me and asking a simple question, "What's on your mind, Jim?"

I took a deep breath and said the words I had rehearsed in my mind countless times over the past few days.

"Walter, I've been here for six years and I'm really not happy. Sometimes, I wonder if what we are doing has any effect at all. I often ask myself if I can do this for the rest of my life."

At the age of twenty-seven, walking into my boss's office and telling him that I thought our work might be meaningless was probably not a smart career move on my part. With any boss other than Walter, I'm certain my move would have met with a few dismissive comments and relegation to a dead-end position in the company.

But I was lucky.

Walter was a rare type of executive which we didn't see much of in the early 1970s. He was an enlightened man who believed in bringing out the best in his employees and taking a few risks along the way. He considered my statement, took a deep breath, and then asked me a question that changed my life.

"Well, Jim . . . what do you want to do about it?"

That question launched the most important process in my life—a process that continues to this day. Walter and I talked at length about my concerns. I left his office with a plan. I would take some time during my workday to meet with others in the field to learn what they were doing and whether my career path was comparable. I started with school friends and people I had met at conferences or business events. I called them up and, surprisingly, they were more than willing to meet with me.

My conversations revealed two things. First, the positions available at other workplaces were very similar to mine; therefore, if I wanted something different or new, it would involve a significant change for me. More importantly, I learned about an entirely new world outside of my workplace, a discovery that led me to later change jobs and begin a career that has been an ongoing exercise in self-discovery.

In the decades since then, I have had a remarkable career. I moved on from the bank to become an executive search consultant, working my way up to become a partner in a large international consulting firm. From there, I created my own business associated with a leading boutique consulting firm. I now head up an international executive search consortium, a position that sees me travel from Singapore to Paris to India and all points in between. As I have built my practice, I developed a growing executive coaching business that has given me the opportunity to meet not only a "who's who" of corporate leaders, but also a wide variety of interesting people who are dealing with their own challenges, from high-potential managers, business students, almost-retirees, and other people's kids. It was only when I made the shift to the consulting and coaching world that I truly consider that I began to fully live the principles that would become A.I.M. While Alex was fortunate to have a ready-made method to access, I worked my way through it over the decades, but greatly increased my happiness as a result.

This book is about sharing what I've learned in the last thirty-plus years with anyone who has ever asked if they can do better in any aspect of their life. The approach I will outline through the course of this book is one that I have used and refined with more than 500 people who started by asking the same question as I did.

Where will your own journey end?

Many of the clients I have coached over the years have asked me the same question at the end of the process: "Why didn't I start this earlier in my life?"

I have seen staunch corporate types with latent entrepreneurial talents turn themselves into outstanding owner/managers. I have seen young people start to take charge of their destiny early in their job history. I have seen many people who began the process with low self-esteem who discovered that there was something special about them and went on to capitalize on that quality.

Once you have completed the A.I.M. process, it should lead to a lifelong method of continuous improvement that will lead you places you never could have dreamed of at the outset.

Now, let's get going on your journey and make it happen!

PART I

Why A.I.M. Matters

CHAPTER 1

Making the Choice

By three methods we may learn wisdom: First, by reflection, which is noblest; second, by imitation, which is easiest; and third, by experience, which is the bitterest.

—Confucius

The man sitting across from me was obviously disappointed about something. His eyes, his posture, and the way he had introduced himself to me all conveyed his belief that he had failed at something. And his next words to me confirmed it.

"Jim, I was one of two candidates for CEO of this firm," he said, gesturing at the office around him, both angry and uncertain at the same time. "And they chose the other guy. *Now* what the heck do I do?"

This was my first meeting with Joe, the president of a global services company. He had called me at my office a few weeks previously at the recommendation of one of his colleagues, to discuss executive coaching help. Now I was sitting across from him in his well-appointed office in the heart of the financial district.

Joe's office told a different story than the one he was telling me. From its size and location—and the several staff who ushered me into the inner sanctum—he was obviously important to the firm. Tasteful art hung on the walls and a couple of smiling family photos were some of the few personal touches in evidence. Had he not begun to confide in me, I would have thought he was a man in command of his own life—a man on top of the world.

But I was not sitting in his office because of what I—or others around him—might have thought. I was there because he was grappling with what he saw as an inexplicable failure. It was my job to help him gain some perspective on his current situation—and move forward.

As I do with every new client, I began by asking him a few general opening questions. When I reached, "Tell me about yourself" he really began to open up to me.

It always amazes me how this simple, yet powerful, leading statement unlocks so many doors with so many people. With Joe, his frustration and worry came pouring out. He told me about his disappointment at not being picked as CEO in a competitive process. He had worked for this company for most of his adult life, he explained, and now felt rejected by it and uncertain of his future.

I encouraged him to talk further about his life and his accomplishments. The story Joe related was typical of the many high-performing, high-achieving executives that I have coached over the years. He talked about his competitive nature and how he had always done well in sports. He spoke of his love for the outdoors and the pride he took in his family's accomplishments. Joe related how his career path had been a steady ascent to the highest rungs of the corporate world, with glowing endorsements from his employer and respect from his colleagues.

As he trailed off, Joe looked at me, defiantly, as if to say that he couldn't understand how he had been turned down for the CEO position, as that decision by his firm simply didn't fit his pattern of success.

As is often the case with coaching, it was now my turn to challenge him a little with the pattern—and the conclusion—I saw emerging.

"Joe," I said, "what you are really telling me is that this is the first time you have ever lost in your life."

There was absolute silence in the room as he glared at me. It was obvious that I had hit a nerve. "You son of a gun," he said, with a bit of a smile now coming to his face, "you are the first person who has got this right with me."

With that, we were off and running.

In the following months, Joe and I were able to move quickly through the various stages of the A.I.M. coaching method because we had identified his real issue very early in the process. Together, we looked deep inside Joe at what he really valued, helping him identify his key positive and negative attributes. I gave him various tools and asked him to examine how he felt about staying with his company versus beginning to think of another life beyond it. He began to develop his external network to consider other options and solicit different perspectives on his skills and challenges.

As Joe's executive coach, I counseled him in a supportive way, helping him define his direction, occasionally asking provocative questions, and serving as a sounding board for his ideas and thoughts. My journey with him came to a successful conclusion several months after I had first sat across from him in his office and confronted him with his first failure. Our discussions over the preceding months had led him to a fork in the road. While he was dedicated to the company to which he had devoted so much of his time and energy, he had discovered a new and exciting world beyond that company where he thought he could make a difference. I challenged Joe again, asking him—based on the high regard I knew he had for his family—what would they advise him to do at this point in his life?

With only a moment's thought, Joe blurted out, "Well, they'd tell me to move on!"

He paused after speaking, as if he couldn't believe he had said those words. And then he began smiling.

I did not have to say anything more. Through our work together, Joe had—without really realizing it—figured out his next move to the point that it was now obvious to him.

When he shared this realization with his colleagues, they were not surprised. They worked with Joe to arrange an appropriate exit strategy and Joe was able to leave on good terms with the company to which he had devoted so much of his life. In the following year, he moved on to become the CEO of one of his original firm's major clients. Joe was happier than anyone had seen him in years. The process we had undertaken together allowed him to discover what he truly valued, and he had achieved a state of self-fulfillment and discovered a new sense of passion about his career and life.

Joe's story is an example of what a good executive coaching process can achieve for someone who is confronted with a challenge that they just aren't able to quite see their way through.

A lack of self-fulfillment in their careers and an absence of passion about life are the two prevailing complaints that I hear from my coaching clients.

In most cases, it starts with a feeling of despair, hopelessness, or even guilt about not being able to control their destiny. Often, clients talk about how alone they feel, telling stories of barely controlling their emotions around co-workers and family in the face of such a challenge. Again and again, I have seen very successful and motivated people brought to the depths of despair by a challenge that they simply can't overcome.

Most people do not find it easy to admit weakness or expose their vulnerability. Even with their closest friends, people like to keep up a facade of control and competence. In private moments, when a coaching relationship begins to click, however, a client's reserve often crumbles and they confess, for the first time, how vulnerable they really feel. Emotions and reactions come tumbling out, as professionals who are normally accustomed to being in control begin to admit that they have found an issue that even they cannot move beyond. Just as Joe, who had always been on an upward track, conquering every obstacle, was finally confronted with a situation he could not overcome, most of my clients reach a point where they realize they simply can't do it on their own.

The big news is that my coaching clients have *all* faced this initial stage of vulnerability and a resistance to sharing when trying to get their heads around a significant career or life challenge.

I had this same experience when I first met with my own executive coach decades ago. Alex, my co-author, went through this situation when he was my coaching client, sitting across a table from me confessing how he felt about his life and career. We are both fortunate, albeit at different stages in our lives, to have found our passions in life and the ability to manage our own destinies. Using the method outlined in this book, Alex moved quickly from a middle-management position early in his career, to a career path that is rewarding and makes him happy. I found my passion as a career coach at the age of fifty-two, and now, ten years later, I am proud to be able to share this very practical approach not just with individual clients—but with every reader of this book.

I am writing this book because the A.I.M. process can work for everyone—not just CEOs and senior executives. Anyone can, with a systematic approach, the right questions, the right exercises, and the right roadmap, look beyond their challenges to find a new place in their life. Coaching *can* be that transformational.

Through this book I am sharing what I've learned in the last thirty-plus years with anyone who has ever asked if they can do better in any aspect of their life. The method that I will outline is one that I have used and refined with more than 500 individuals across many generations, who started in the same place as Joe. And it has worked—to varying degrees—for each of them.

In the chapters that follow, you will move through a thorough process that—if followed correctly—can help you face and overcome your challenges. In the following pages, I will share many real-life stories of people who faced similar challenges to those you now face and overcame them with the help of my coaching method.

The A.I.M. process does not offer an easy fix. But you already know that. You know that if changing your life or overcoming significant challenges was easy to do, more people would do it, and more people would become self-fulfilled and realize their passion about life. What this book does is demystify this transformation, breaking it down into manageable steps that can take a person from despair and hopelessness to a point where they discover their true passion in life and become self-fulfilled.

If you see that helplessness in yourself—and want to reach a point of self-determination and passion—read on.

Now let's get started!

CHAPTER 2

What Makes People Happy, Really?

Happiness is essentially a state of going somewhere, wholeheartedly, one-directionally, without
regret or reservation.

—William H. Sheldon

Happiness. What is it, really?

People talk a lot about happiness. Countless books have been written, hours and hours of thinking by great philosophers, and reams of poetry and prose have been dedicated to examining what will make human beings happy. Daytime talk shows go over the countless aspects of whether people are happy and, if not, why not? The plots of films and television shows revolve around the pursuit of love, money, power, and relationships with one root motivation— if the characters achieve their goals, they will somehow be happier and more complete. The advertising industry tries to convince us that the next house, a better car, or a different product will somehow make us happier. Even the constitution of the United States, the gov-erning document of the most powerful and progressive society in the world, enshrines the "pursuit of happiness" as a core principle for its citizens.

You would think that with such a preoccupation with happiness throughout human history, with the aim of increasing happiness at the core of many of our leisure, professional, and political activities, that people would be . . . well . . . happier. But that doesn't seem to be the case. Most, if not all, of the people I coach through the A.I.M. process are not happy at the beginning. These are generally professional people who occupy important positions in the corporate hierarchy. They are, generally, CEOs or up-and-coming executives—people who, to all outside observers, are at the top of their game, full of promise, and primed for achievement. Yet, when you get down to it, they all come to the A.I.M. process because they are looking for something that will make them happier.

When I ask the question that starts all these clients through the A.I.M. process, "Tell me about yourself," they often reel off their accomplishments, give me a summary of their resumés, or highlight things they think will impress me. As we will see in the coming chapters, that's completely acceptable at the starting stages of A.I.M. No one has to be completely self-aware and get it "right" at the starting gate. When I explore why they are looking for an executive coach and what they are hoping to achieve through the A.I.M. process, however, a different story begins to emerge. They talk about some unmet need, some concern they may have that what they are doing now may not be the best fit for them. In most cases, they are not yet aware of *why* they feel this way—only that they do feel unhappy.

Wait a minute, you might say. People who are outwardly successful, people who seem to have everything going for them can be just as unhappy as the rest of us? Yes, that is exactly what I am saying. Throughout this book, you will meet examples drawn from my practice of people who started the A.I.M. process with a lot going for them. For some reason, however, they were looking for something else—something that, in most cases, they could not define at the start. They knew they were unhappy and wanted to move to address it, but they didn't know how, or even what they could do about it.

That is why so many successful people have taken so quickly to the A.I.M. process. They needed a method that understood their starting point, helping them identify what they were trying to focus on, exploring why they felt that way and what they valued about their life and career, and then put them on the road to doing something about it.

Often, the mistake that many of them make at the start of the process is that a simple transition or a change of environment will "fix" their vague feelings of unhappiness. "All I need," any of them might say at the beginning, "is a new job just like this one, but at a different firm." Others think that a small change of scenery—a different town, a new neighborhood, a new property, or relationship will somehow address something that, once we explore it, rests unseen within their circumstance and directly affects their capacity to be happy. The root causes of why people are unhappy run deep, and cannot, generally, be solved with a simple change in salary, employer, or other superficial factors. The road to happiness starts with a strong degree of self-knowledge about why you do the things you do, awareness about your values, and about the things that motivate you. At the end of that journey, it involves you taking that new self-awareness and applying it to your professional or personal life in a way that ensures you are spending your time doing things that you truly want to do.

Sound simple? Well, not really. But understanding what is at the heart of human happiness makes the journey through the A.I.M. process possible.

Learning from the example of happy people

We all know happy people, don't we? Throughout our lives, we are often blessed when we meet people who seem to have it all. This is not to say that they are more materially successful than others or more powerful or better looking or have a better professional or personal position. We have all met people who somehow exude a calm, confident enjoyment about life, as if they are completely and genuinely comfortable with who they are and what they are doing. There isn't any hint of meanness or reserve or of a hidden agenda in such people. They are generally outward looking, able to engage and talk about life and their work or families, and are completely at ease with themselves and with others. They, more often than not, have a giving orientation, ready to help others succeed without a hint of reservation or reluctance. Their professional and personal lives are usually full and vibrant. They do interesting things, know interesting people, are committed to their relationships and families, and generally exude a modest feeling of being on top of their game without a hint of judgment or of competition. Comfortable in who they are, they make others feel at ease and inspire them with their example without even trying.

When you are fortunate enough to meet such people, you often come away saying, "Wow, she was a great person. I wonder how she does it?" Many people find themselves in such positions naturally. They have found that ideal combination of self-awareness that keeps them grounded, a job that reflects their values, temperament, and personal circumstances that support their ability to grow personally and professionally. The purpose behind A.I.M., however, is to help those people for whom this does not happen naturally or accidentally, to move their own lives in this direction.

In all my decades of coaching, I have encountered only a handful of people who were so on top of their game that I concluded they would probably not benefit in some way from the A.I.M. method. One of the best examples was Vitali, an engineer from Eastern Europe who was referred to me by a former colleague. Vitali was in his early forties, married with two children, and, at the time, was working in a mid-level position at an information systems firm that worked with high-profile healthcare clients.

We met on a cool autumn day in a coffee shop near his office. He was waiting for me when I arrived 10 minutes early and, after our initial pleasantries, we quickly established a rapport. He spoke in a confident and unhurried manner about his career path and his technical expertise in management information systems. It was clear that he was comfortable in his job and liked what he did for a living. After about 20 minutes of conversation, I felt I had to ask why he felt he needed a coach.

Vitali explained that he had welcomed his colleague's recommendation to talk with me, because his superior, while happy with his track record, was urging him to think "outside of the box" and develop new ideas for his department. "I'm not sure if I'm good with this kind of stuff," he explained, "so I wanted someone to offer me a second opinion. And I hear you function well as a 'devil's advocate.'"

I was a little flattered, so I listened intently as he sketched out the challenges his company was facing and the ideas he had developed to respond to them. Specifically, he had developed an approach that would see him heading up a new business unit for his firm, and he had mapped out how he might present this new strategy to his boss. As he walked me through his thinking, I saw that his plan was well thought out—covering the strategic need, and backed by solid financial projections and an appreciation of the risks. There was little I could offer, I told him, in the way of advice to improve his approach. However, there was one aspect with which I thought I might be able to help him.

"Vitali," I asked him, "if you are successful with this, how do you think heading up this new unit would impact your family life?"

He smiled and with genuine emotion said, "If this goes through, I will be the happiest person in the world. My wife and I have talked about it and we are confident that it will mean only good things for us."

With that I shook his hand and smiled back. "I'm happy to say that there is nothing I think I can do for you, Vitali," I said. "Just be sure to let me know how it turns out."

Three days later, I received a polite e-mail from Vitali, thanking me for listening to him. His boss had responded positively to his proposal and had given the green light to the new business unit—and to his promotion!

For every Vitali, there have been hundreds of people like Kate—people who have all the ingredients to become happier and more fulfilled, and managed to do so through the A.I.M. process. Moreover, Kate's example shows that—unlike many of my clients—you often do not have to undertake huge changes in your work and professional life to make significant progress in your happiness quotient.

Kate was an up-and-coming executive in the financial services field, referred to me by her CEO. He sent me a cryptic e-mail asking if I would meet with Kate and consider taking her on as a coaching client. "She's fantastic," his e-mail read, "she just doesn't realize it yet. See if you can help her."

My curiosity was piqued by this introduction, and I arranged to meet with Kate early the following week. The young woman who met me in my office was in her mid-thirties with straight brown hair and a conservative business suit—someone who would not have attracted much attention in any of the thousands of firms within walking distance of my office. Yet, as we began to talk, I found her to be incredibly enthusiastic, cheery, and engaging. She was one of those rare types that others euphemistically call a "people person." It was obvious from how she made small talk with me that she genuinely cared about what I had to say, and her obvious charisma and interest in my questions only reaffirmed my initial perception.

As we talked, Kate matter-of-factly related her career accomplishments to date. She had come from a modest family and had completed her MBA, supported by scholarships, at the age of twenty-six. After a few positions in the finance industry, she had been recruited as a junior VP in her bank and was already working on some high-profile projects that had brought her to the attention of the CEO. As I questioned her about some of these projects, she calmly, and without any hint of self-promotion, told me that they had all come in on time, under budget, and had made a significant contribution to the overall performance of the firm.

"I guess they all worked out alright," she said with a shrug, "but I don't think they were anything special."

When I pointed out to her that, in other businesses, such achievements from someone at such an early stage in her career would be seen as quite exceptional, she was clearly uncomfortable with the praise I was offering. "That's what they hired me for, Jim," she replied. "I'm just doing my job."

With this, I began to understand what her CEO had meant in his e-mail. It was becoming obvious to me as we talked, that Kate didn't think she was anything special. Despite her charisma, her ability to relate well with others, and the fact that she had led several high-profile projects to successful outcomes, Kate was naturally self-effacing and understated. While endearing personal qualities, if taken too far in a corporate environment, they could be fatal to her career.

Something had driven her to ask her firm to support her with a coach, however, so that is where I directed our conversation. As we explored why she thought she needed a coach, she was initially a little evasive, saying, "Others thought it was a good idea," or "They say all people can benefit from coaching at some point in their careers." When I pushed her a little further, however, Kate dropped her guard and she began to share with me how she really felt about her professional life. She was clearly happy and enthusiastic about her job, but felt less optimistic about her career path at the bank. While her projects had, so far, been successful, she was encountering negative feedback from some of her colleagues who, although she seemed unaware of it, were apparently jealous of her success. One colleague, in particular, had outmaneuvered her for a new project, leaving a bad taste in her mouth. She clearly felt uncomfortable with the office politics that surrounded her current position.

"Maybe I'm overreacting, Jim," she said, "but maybe not. I would like to stay with the bank, but have a bit more control over what I do so I can avoid the politics. I feel like I've been doing what everyone has wanted me to do and I'd rather work on things that I want to."

I find with many of my clients that office politics are an unavoidable part of what makes them unhappy about their jobs, as well as a certain lack of control over their workloads and career directions. Others, who tend to focus on issues other than the task at hand or who get too involved in the day-to-day operations of a project, most often to its detriment, often stymie people who are high achieving or have great potential. I had no doubt with Kate, however, that her problem could likely be fixed in a short amount of time. She was not looking to make a major change in her professional life and, from her CEO's endorsement and what I observed in the way she dealt with me, we had a very solid base upon which to build.

In the weeks that followed, Kate and I worked through the stages of the A.I.M. process, helping her identify her strengths and weaknesses, her values, and what truly made her happy. The deeper we delved into these self-awareness exercises, the more she came to the understanding that she was a perfect fit for the bank at this point in her career. Moreover, as we moved into the more outward-looking phases of A.I.M., she had the good fortune of identifying a new position within her organization that seemed to be the answer for many of her issues with her current position. It was a more senior VP position that would build on her previous successes and it offered a greater degree of independence from the office politics that she had identified as a problem. By putting the emphasis on personal networking from A.I.M.'s later stages to good use inside her firm, she was able to connect with potential sponsors in other parts of the organization and secure the new position. I met her for coffee a few weeks after she had taken on her new job and found her even more engaged and dynamic than I had at our first meeting.

The new position offered a big boost for her self-confidence, and the feedback she received through the hiring process had allowed her to begin to understand why the bank had valued her contribution. While this small change in her work environment had made Kate even more secure and happier, I know she will put the principles of A.I.M. to good use as she continues to develop both professionally and personally.

Is happiness attainable? What the research tells us

While anecdotes offer us clues to what may make people happier, what do we really know about human happiness? Surely, after millennia of discussing and thinking about the issue, we should have some relatively solid insight into what makes human beings truly happy? Thousands of pages of medical and academic journals have been devoted to some aspect of happiness studies over the years, but it is only recently that we have begun to find common factors among people who would fit the example of happiness we offered at the start of the chapter.

One of the most significant questions we can address right off the bat would be whether it is possible to "manage" one's life to attain happiness. Put another way, is the ability to be happy just part of who we are, or can we actively shape our lives to make ourselves happier? The answer to that question would seem to be obvious. Haven't we dedicated entire segments of society towards helping people become happier? Whether it is the fields of psychiatry or psychology, the burgeoning field of self-help books, groups, and methods or even the assumptions behind most of the advertisements we see each day, we have assumed, as a society, that happiness is something that, with the right effort, can be manufactured.

When we review the research, however, the picture gets a little more complicated than one would think. One of the seminal books in this field is *The How of Happiness* by University of California psychologist Sona Lyubomisky. From her research, she proposed that up to 50 percent of a person's ability to be happy is determined by genetics. We are predisposed to have a certain "set point" of happiness that, no matter what happens to us, we always fall back to. This brings to mind the example of the lottery winner who, after some initial euphoria at her winnings, settles back into the same pessimistic view of life she had prior to her win. Or, on a more positive note, a person who might suffer a significant setback but, once he has digested it, returns to the same optimistic outlook he had before.

Of the remaining 50 percent potential of a person to be happy, Lyubomisky writes, 10 percent is the product of your life circumstances and situation—whether you live in a cardboard box under a freeway or in a nice condo, for example. The final 40 percent of your capability to be happy, however, is firmly within your outlook and self-control.

What does this mean, practically? Those reading Lyubomisky's work often jump at the fact that half of your potential to be happy is determined by genetics and upbringing—things completely beyond your control. At least 40 percent of your potential to be happy, however, is totally within your control and, if you can find a way to maximize your happiness through your own actions, you stand a good chance of dealing with the other 10 percent that comes from your present circumstances. Put another way, if you can find it within yourself to manage those things you can control which affect your happiness, you can also impact your economic and material circumstances that play a role in making you happy.

Other research has followed large numbers of people over long periods of time, to find out what makes them happy. Perhaps the most comprehensive study in this regard is the Harvard Study of Adult Development. Beginning in 1937, this study has followed more than two hundred men through their lives, carefully measuring what happens to them and—more interestingly—trying to figure out why some had good outcomes in their lives while others did not.

Some of the study's findings offer little surprise to us as we sit firmly in the 21st century, but they were groundbreaking at the time. Participants who drank to excess and smoked heavily, for example, had poorer health outcomes than those who did not. Being well-educated led to better economic and psychological outcomes, as did the ability to maintain a stable relationship. Moderate exercise and healthy eating had a mildly beneficial effect.

Beyond what we would now consider to be obvious findings, however, lie some interesting insights into the role of how participants dealt with their challenges and their overall happiness. The study's curator, George Vaillant, stresses that the ability of participants to successfully adapt to hardship was one of greatest predictors of their overall success in life. Participants who used appropriate "defense mechanisms" to adapt to change were more likely to have good outcomes than those who did not. And while there were complex factors surrounding the ability of people to adapt, the single biggest predictor identified by Vaillant was their use of social relationships. "The only thing that really matters in life," Valliant went as far as to say in a 2009 interview with *The Atlantic*, "are your relationships to other people." The ability of people to maintain strong social connections with family, friends, and professional colleagues was very important in their ability to handle the challenges that life threw at them.

Can things make us happier?

In any discussion of happiness, the issue usually arises of whether achieving certain material goals can actually make people happier. Does that new house, car, or vacation property really make you happier? The short answer is yes—and no. Research tells us that obtaining something we want can lead to a short-term spike in happiness, but that we quickly revert to the level of happiness that we had before—the happiness "set point" noted earlier.

This is not to say that material wealth does not make us happy. Research has also shown, quite obviously, that we require a certain level of possessions to be self-sufficient and free from basic material want. We need, for example, an apartment, house, or condo in which to live, but once that basic need is met, moving to a much bigger or more opulent dwelling does not result in a significant improvement in happiness. The same holds true for clothing, food, or any other comparable material possession: Once we have met our basic needs, we do not get exponentially happier when we obtain more beyond that point.

So if things only bring us momentary happiness, what makes us happier in the long term? While there is no definitive answer to this question, there are studies that strongly indicate that it is the ability of people to exercise control over their own personal and professional lives that contributes greatly to long-term happiness.

Timothy Judge, a management guru at the University of Florida, has spent considerable time researching what he calls "core self-evaluations" and their link to personal and professional success. While his work builds on the considerable attention that has been spent in the area of self-esteem, his concept of self-evaluation goes far beyond feeling good about oneself. His basic theory, backed by considerable research, is that people succeed when they have the strong belief that they are competent, when they are generally open and optimistic that "life will turn out well," and believe that they are in control of their own lives. Judge then goes on to propose that, if we can find ways to encourage and reinforce these core beliefs in people, they will achieve more positive outcomes in their lives than those who do not.

Intuitively, this makes sense. It takes little imagination or theorizing to think how having little faith in your own abilities or living at the whims of the decisions of others could make someone unhappy. While no person is wholly in command of his or her life at all times, imagine for a moment that you had little or no control over what happened to you. Imagine if your job consisted of waiting for someone to tell you exactly what to do, looking over your shoulder and pointing out when you were not doing something correctly. If you had next to no latitude to make decisions about your job, it doesn't sound like a recipe for happiness, does it? Now imagine the reverse—you are making decisions that determine the direction that your life takes. You feel comfortable in what you are doing and, by increasingly challenging yourself and successfully meeting those challenges—or learning from the occasional mistake—you have built your confidence to a point where you no longer fear failure. Initiative and engagement are your natural inclinations. And when something happens that you did not expect, your immediate reaction is not to ask, "Why did that happen to me?" but to think, "Okay, now what can I do about that?"

One orientation leads to helplessness, and helplessness leads to disappointment and unhappiness. The other orientation leads to resiliency, to initiative, and—eventually—to happiness.

Which road would you prefer to take?

It is this conclusion that makes happiness research relevant to the A.I.M. process. If you can find a way to increase the amount of control you have over your professional and personal life, if you can equip yourself with tools and a method that will move you towards taking control and ensuring that you maintain control as you move forward through life, this should make you a happier person down the road.

A life in control: Anna's story

One of the main challenges facing female executives of any generation is breaking the "glass ceiling" that keeps many women out of the most senior positions. While this remains a popular theme in the career field today, it was a much more serious challenge back in the mid-1970s when I first met Anna. At the time, I had not yet developed my coaching practice and was still working exclusively as an executive search consultant, helping recruit and place executives for firms around the world. Anna was one of those successful candidates. In her late-twenties, I helped recruit her for a senior position in a marketing research firm, where she benefitted from what was a rarity at the time—a male CEO who was committed to mentoring and promoting qualified female executives.

As she moved towards the executive ranks in the following years, Anna kept in touch with me and our relationship eventually morphed into a coaching arrangement. She was beginning the A.I.M. method from a position of strength. She was already experienced in the executive suite and was quite poised, articulate, and forthright. She did not back down when challenged on her principles and was very skilled at asserting herself in the face of many of her less-enlightened male colleagues.

As she worked through the rigors of the A.I.M. process, Anna moved on to become the first female vice president in her firm and one of a limited number in the entire country. We remained in close contact over the years as she continued to achieve and put A.I.M.'s principles into action. Often, she would come to me for advice or counsel about an internal challenge she was facing, and at other times, just to chat and update me on her progress. She took particularly well to the networking emphasis in the later stages of A.I.M., as she had developed quite a broad range of contacts across a number of industries, nonprofit organizations, and throughout government and political circles. Through it all, she was able to find an amazing life partner and raise a wonderful daughter with him.

Today, Anna and I are still in touch. She has moved through a succession of senior positions, serves on the board of directors for a number of firms, and is a mentor and inspiration to an entirely new generation of female executives, with whom she generously shares her time and knowledge. Continuing to give back what the process has given her, she is a true A.I.M. success story. As I reflect on the progress she made, I would have to say that Anna represents the best of what A.I.M. can help a person to achieve—self-awareness, confidence, career and personal success, and the ability to give back to those who can benefit from your example and experience.

Moving forward through the A.I.M. method

The following chapters of this book have but one purpose: To help you address whatever challenge you are facing and to point you in the direction of becoming one of the happy, fulfilled people we have talked about in the preceding pages.

Doing this will take commitment on your part to follow the method thoroughly. It is human nature to want to "cut to the chase" and start fixing things right away. As you move through the A.I.M. method, resist that impulse as strongly as you can. I have successfully used this method to coach hundreds of executives around the world and, in the small number of instances where it hasn't produced results to my satisfaction and that of my coaching client, it has been due to the client short-circuiting the process.

A.I.M. relies in large part on laying a solid foundation of self-awareness in the first few steps. Before you run off and try to do something, this method teaches that you first have to know yourself better. You have to learn about what motivates you, what values you are bringing to the table, what patterns have played out over the various decades of your life, and what future options you might explore to address the challenge you have. Be sure to take the time the method prescribes to complete those initial self-awareness stages—and then move through the remaining ones in sequence.

By the end of the A.I.M. process, we hope that you will be well on your way to becoming the type of person that you have met in this chapter—people who are moving forward, happy with their direction in life and their ability to make change happen. These individuals are not on the receiving end of the capricious whims of employers or others, but are truly empowered about making choices with respect to their own lives. People who, when challenges befall them, have options they can consider and—if their options are not immediately evident—they have a way of creating their own. If you are successful in reaching this direction, the final stage of A.I.M. notes that you can become an agent of change not just for your own life and its challenges, but you can also become both a resource to help others and an example from whom they can learn. Done properly, you can become one of the people we write about in this book.

Good luck with your journey. And remember, A.I.M. high!

PART II

The 10-Step Process

CHAPTER 3

(Un)Willing and Able? Starting Your Journey through the A.I.M. Process

If you do not change direction, you may end up where you are heading.
—Lao Tzu, Chinese philosopher

Everyone talks about change. Just take a moment to count the number of times you, or someone around you, starts a sentence with some version of "wouldn't if be great if . . . ?" Our desire for improvement, for forward motion, is widespread because we are all creatures of change. As a species, we have grown and survived over the millennia because of our constant spirit of questioning, self-improvement, invention, and innovation. On a personal level, the first few decades of our lives are years of gradual progression and continual change. We grow physically. The way we see the world changes as our outlook matures. We progress through an education system that expands our minds and gives us, along with our families and peers, knowledge and skills we carry through the rest of our lives.

But for some reason, as adults, many of us stop making change happen and shift merely to talking and thinking about it. The desire for a better life, a more rewarding career, a different place and circumstance for our families and ourselves is still there. But actually *acting* to change things—especially in a major way—becomes overwhelming for many of us.

And this resistance to change does not rest simply with the individual. If it were easy to change businesses, management consultants would not be so busy. If it were easy to change governments and their policies, politics would not generate such intense attention and require so much commitment from so many people. If it were easy to change the way people behave, marketers would not have to invest such large amounts in advertising, polling, and focus groups. And if individuals found it easy to change themselves, more people would be happier and fewer people would read books such as this one.

Changing yourself is difficult because it often seems like an insurmountable task. We feel the need to move beyond where we are, but any decisions we might make, any courses of action we might plot, are tied up in a flood of self-defeating questions. Am I happy now—and would I be happier if I did something else? What else could I do? Am I fooling myself in thinking I can change? Isn't it risky? Shouldn't I just settle for what I have? And how would I even start the process anyway?

This resistance to change, the seemingly insurmountable challenge of translating our desire for something better into a path that will take us there, is why the first stage of the A.I.M. process is the most difficult. The first stage involves getting all of your issues out into the light of day where you can assess them. It requires honesty, perspective, and the willingness to face difficult truths that many of us prefer to keep hidden.

Knowing how and where to start: Jack's story

Jack called me on a hot summer afternoon. He explained that he was a friend of a former business partner of mine and had been discussing some personal challenges with him. During their conversation, my partner recognized that Jack might benefit from some focused help. "I have a colleague who is a coach who specializes in career issues," he told Jack. "You should give him a call."

In our initial phone conversation, I learned that Jack was a business development manager for a major bank which specialized in small business lending. He had begun to work in banking after business school and had been with his current employer for five years. To an outside observer, Jack was doing well. His employer was satisfied with his work. His executive position earned him a decent salary with annual bonuses that allowed Jack and his wife to live a good life and create a supportive environment for their two children.

There was one major problem, however. Jack felt that his career had stalled and he had no idea how to kick-start it. In our initial conversation, he began to mention some of the same things I hear from many of my clients. "I am not excited to go to work anymore, Jim," he said. "My work has become just a job that interests me less and less every day. The bank only seems to care about measurement—and I really don't care about that."

I had an opening in my schedule the following week, so I invited Jack to my home office to continue our chat. When he finally settled into the chair opposite my desk, I found myself talking with a man in his mid-thirties who was wearing a rumpled suit and looking somewhat harried. I could sense he was uneasy and a little nervous, as if he were doing something disloyal to his employer, so I tried to put him at ease.

As we began chatting, I found Jack to be gregarious with a good sense of humor. While he tried to take control of the conversation at first, his story meandered all over the map and he quickly ran out of things to say and couldn't succinctly articulate what was bugging him. When I asked him to "Tell me about yourself," he didn't know where to start. Instead, he veered into bravado, talking about his achievements and how his annual glowing performance reviews assured him that his employer thought he had a great future with the organization.

When I probed him more to discuss his relationship with the bank, the truth gradually began to emerge. His employer had begun to restructure, eliminating levels of management and reducing the distance between those in the executive ranks and those on the front lines. While this was supposed to lead to a more efficient corporate structure that would better engage supposed high achievers such as Jack, it had the unintended consequence of limiting the number of opportunities that would allow him to move into the executive suite. As Jack was explaining this career bottleneck, I asked him a simple question.

"Jack, you say you want to move ahead, but I have to ask you this: Do you want to stay at this organization? If there was an opportunity for a promotion, would you take it?"

He immediately began to say yes, but stopped himself, realization dawning on his face.

"To tell you the truth, Jim, I'm not sure that I want to stay in the company given what it is starting to look like. But I'm not sure what I would do if I left the financial services industry. Maybe it is time to think about a career shift, but honestly," he leaned in and lowered his voice, "I have no idea how to begin that process or where I might want to go."

At this point, I smiled. "Jack, many of the people I've helped say exactly the same thing. My method can help you. Now let's get to work."

Starting the A.I.M. process: Getting it all out ...

It is tough to start a journey when you don't know your objective or where you are going. Many people find it easy to talk about their unhappiness, but are paralyzed with the sense they are unable to act to improve their situation. To help people get moving is a core function of the A.I.M. method—and it begins with "getting it all out."

Jack had taken a major step by admitting that he was unsure about his present circumstances—he did not know how he could move ahead. This was a difficult realization for a high achiever like Jack to make. On the surface, his "story" was a good one. He was a successful executive, valued by his company, with a good family and limitless prospects. But when he finally let his guard down and began confessing some of his doubts, he felt alone, somewhat mad at himself, and bitter at his situation.

"Am I the only one who feels like this?" he asked at one point. "Have any of your other clients felt this way? What are my options to get past this?" His confession led to a breakthrough in our coaching relationship. When I assured him that others in his situation have had similar feelings, and that such emotions are not a confession of weakness, he visibly relaxed. From that point forward, we moved past his bravado and defense mechanisms and began to progress to the first stage of the A.I.M. process: Getting all his issues out, and, in the cold light of day, discussing whether he was willing to explore them.

Six steps to capturing, understanding, and moving forward

Human beings, when they finally begin to consider making changes or moving forward, often jump into action right away. The A.I.M. process begins not with action, but with reflection. This flows from a simple premise: You can't fix something if you don't know what the problem(s) is or what your options are to fix it.

The first stage of A.I.M., therefore, begins with a series of steps to draw out your issues in a format that allows you to take a rational look at them.

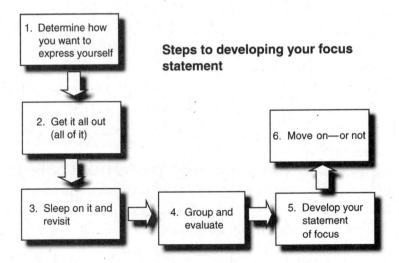

Step One: Determine how you want to express yourself

The major objective in this phase of the A.I.M. process is to express all of your issues, to take all your anxieties, fears, and ideas and get them out of your brain and into the light of day. Once you have listed them somewhere, you can begin to look at them rationally and ask yourself some potentially difficult, but important, questions.

Before you start "downloading," determine how you want to capture your ideas.

There are many ways to do this. For people who like to write, they can just put pen to paper or type away on their computer. For others who are more verbal, talking it out makes sense, either with a trusted friend or to a voice recorder.

Determine what method works best for you, and then move to step two of the process.

Step Two: Get it all out (all of it)

Sitting in front of your computer screen, voice recorder, or blank pad of paper, spend a few moments thinking about how you feel about the challenge that has led you to this book. Then, let your thoughts flow, with no hesitation. Your objective here is to capture your underlying, base feelings, un-moderated by analysis, context or second thoughts. Disregard any instinct you have to extend or elaborate on your thoughts with statements that begin with "but..." or "what if...?"

You don't have to worry about the order in which your thoughts come out or whether others can understand them. This stage is about unloading what you have been carrying for some time, so simply focus on getting it out. Remember, if you think too hard about how you feel, you will experience the same feeling of confusion that Jack went through initially which prevented him from articulating his problems.

Many people find this phase difficult. Unstructured thinking, writing, or speaking is not something we do regularly. Jack faced the same challenge when we moved on to framing his issues. In our conversation, he began with the current state of his career and his raw feelings about that. He then explained what he saw changing in the organization and what he felt would stay the same, noting his initial unfiltered thoughts about the impact of these changes on him. Jack then moved on to his very emotional reaction to what he perceived as his loss of energy and motivation. He went further, expressing the doubts he had about his future. Ultimately, he concluded with a very revealing description of his total frustration and lack of self-esteem.

While Jack was able to open up because he was talking with me, you can have your own moments of self-discovery with the right approach and frame of mind. If you are having difficulty starting your "download" or expressing yourself, consider the following statements or questions that have served as "door openers" for other clients of mine. Choose one of the following that is most appropriate for you, and then let your mind wander spontaneously from that starting point:

- Am I happy right now? If not, why?
- Say or write one thing, spontaneously, that finishes the statement "I am not fulfilled right now because . . ."
- I feel I should get on with my life—what does that look like for me?
- My career is in a rut and I don't know what to do.
- I am paid to do and not to think—and I like to think.
- Nobody cares what I do—and I don't care about my job.
- My colleagues are passing me by.
- My industry is changing and I don' know what to do; I am not sure I want to be in it anymore.
- I want to do something that I am passionate about.

Remember that there are no "correct" thoughts at this stage. What is important to you is important—so get it out. All of it.

Step Three: Sleep on it and revisit

The time you take away from your challenges can be as productive as the time you spend thinking or worrying about them. Often, I have spent hours puzzling over an issue at my desk, staring at my screen, only to have the solution come to me in the shower, in the garden, or while kayaking across a quiet lake.

After you have downloaded all that you think you can, take an evening away from your thoughts and revisit them the next day. Review the material and ask yourself one more time—is there anything that has not been covered?

Step Four: Group and evaluate

If you are satisfied that you have done a good job in outlining your concerns, review them to see if any recurring themes leap off the page.

With Jack, one of the themes we identified was, at several points in his career, his nervous energy had forced him to make a change. From the way he described some of his life transitions, it was clear that he was easily bored, particularly when things became too bureaucratic. Another theme was that he had been competitive in everything he had done in life—from sports, his MBA, his career, and even his family trying to "keep up with the Joneses" in their neighborhood.

Capturing all of these themes in one place was quite revealing to Jack. While it was too early in the A.I.M. process to make these themes part of his change process, it was important to flag them for the work we would do later in the process.

Step Five: Develop your statement of focus

With all of your initial feelings captured in some form, the next step is to develop a statement of focus that builds on these observations.

For Jack, after we had captured all of his raw feelings about his current circumstance, we needed to consolidate all of his feelings and issues into a simple statement of focus. This is a critical step! In the latter stages of the A.I.M. process, when you connect with others and begin to explore your options about your future, you will need to have a clear statement of your issues and objectives that will shape and focus your efforts.

In my discussions with Jack, his initial download revealed something important. It was obvious that his current position was not engaging him and that he was consequently finding it difficult to become energized and enthusiastic about his work. It was also clear from his observations and feelings that he valued a high level of engagement in his job and suffered when it was not present. From this realization, Jack and I developed a clear statement that focused his concerns for this initial stage:

> While I am looking for ways to get re-energized in my own organization, I know very little about the world outside the banking industry, and I need a two-track process that explores my career options inside *and* outside the organization.

For your statement, review your thoughts and common themes and *try to develop one sentence that encapsulates what you think is your issue.* Write a few versions, try different wordings but try to land on one sentence that resonates with you and sums up what you believe you are facing.

Later in the process, you will find that it is critical to be concise and honest about your feelings when you are actually out meeting people and asking for their help in your journey. This will make it easier for someone to ask you questions as well as offer you clues as to how to help. Your brief should be positive and upbeat. I have seen too many situations where an individual speaks as if they are pleading for help and looks to their audience as a savior. Guess what! No one is going to feel sorry for you. You are taking this journey because you want to, and you need to be constructive and objective. For example, in Jack's case, he is not saying he is jumping ship, but he is stating legitimate concerns and expressing a logical reason to look at his options. This concise statement should be no more than a couple of sentences, expressing your current state, followed by what you want to focus on going forward.

With a statement in hand with which you are comfortable, move to the final step of the first stage of the A.I.M. process.

Step Six: Move on—or not

At this point, it's decision time. If you are comfortable that you have identified the main issue at the core of your dissatisfaction, you have to determine whether you are prepared to move forward to explore it. The remainder of the A.I.M. process is based on the idea that individuals, on their own, can only go so far. Truly addressing the concerns you have identified in the first stage involves beginning to share them with others who can help you move forward. With your issues in hand, you should now be prepared to commit to the remainder of the process to address them.

Are you prepared?

In Jack's case, acting on his focus statement in the subsequent stages of A.I.M. involved opening up to people who were outside of his normal banking circle. He had to venture beyond his comfort zone and his overachieving bravado, where he had to confide some of his uncertainties and questions to complete strangers. And in order to proceed, Jack had to be prepared to commit to this course of action. Through the course of a year, he worked through the remaining steps of the A.I.M. process, weathering some ups and downs of self-discovery, and eventually ending up in a much better personal space that would enable him to make a decision about his professional space with confidence.

When it's not so cut and dried: Barb's story

In some cases, my clients already believe they know what their problem is before our first meeting. Many of these cases stem from hyper-achieving executives, who think they have already determined what they need to do and are just looking for the brief "blessing" of a coach, so they can do what they know has to be done.

The problem with this approach is, of course, that it totally devalues any external perspective. If you spend your professional life believing that you are a person with all the answers, starting from a place of self-reflection and shared doubt is often a foreign concept.

The following story about Barb highlights what looked liked a quick diagnosis and prescription, but that was not the case. Fortunately, as you will see, Barb stuck with the A.I.M. process.

Barb was a human resources executive with a consumer packaged goods company. She had completed her Executive MBA and was referred to me by the school's career center. In our first meeting, she was incredibly organized from the first few words. She brought notes, performance appraisals, and a clear statement of what she wanted.

"I want to be more in control of my own destiny!" it read.

At first glance, Barb would seem to be an ideal prospect for the A.I.M. method. In fact, a casual observer would say, "Great—now she can start at Stage Two and not bother with this initial step."

I, however, was skeptical. I asked her a variant of the question that had started me on my journey decades earlier to begin our discussion. "Barb," I said, "being in control of your destiny is an admirable goal. But let me ask you a question. What is it that you want to do, really?"

Her brow furrowed, and then she smiled. "Well, Jim, no one has ever asked me that question, and I don't think I've ever asked myself that question either."

The picture of Barb's life that tumbled out in our subsequent conversation revealed a more complex picture than the uber-organized professional who sat before me. It emerged that she trusted her current employer and knew she had been treated well. She had been promoted several times, moving to different cities and facing creative challenges in every role. Her firm had pegged her as a "big picture" thinker who could get a handle on things very quickly and implement successful solutions. However, Barb was experiencing a growing unease about whether she was in control of her own fate and whether her current situation would ever allow her to achieve this goal.

As we explored this issue, it came out that in her career progression, someone else, someone above her in the corporate hierarchy, had always picked her and moved her into a new position. At no point had Barb identified what she wanted and moved to get it—no one had ever asked her what she wanted to do. When the offers of promotion came, she had been caught up in the thrill of the moment, the flattery, and the very visible accomplishment.

To compound matters, Barb was now facing a personal challenge that directly impacted her work and her sense of career control. Her husband was being transferred to another country and, if she was to follow him, she had to consider the impact of that move on her own career path.

This, in turn, opened up entirely new avenues of exploration. Was her career more important than that of her husband—or vice versa? Were there transfer opportunities available within her existing company? Did she even want to stay in the same line of work, or did the upcoming move offer a chance for her to start anew at something completely different?

What had seemed like a simple professional challenge at the start of our conversation had become much more complex after just a few key questions. And again, this illustrates that you cannot jump straight to the action steps of the A.I.M. method without fully understanding your challenges, your motivations, and what you are trying to fix.

You can also see from Barb's example why people often avoid dealing with their challenges head-on. When presented with an overwhelming series of potential choices, each with their own consequences, many people are simply not equipped to look for the hard truths about themselves and others. As a result, they often avoid making a decision or they jump in one direction or another without a plan—sometimes with disastrous results.

In Barb's case, while things were going well, the impending transfer of her husband created a sense of urgency. Like Jack, she was convinced that to increase her odds of taking control, she had to explore options inside and outside her company.

What I really appreciate about these two stories and most of the others I have experienced is, so often in a person's career, no one asks you what you want to do. Sometimes, there is a tiny section in a performance review document that asks for your view, but how often does that resurface? This telling observation is, I believe, what gets the juices flowing about the A.I.M. method.

Jack's and Barb's stories: A new beginning

Jack followed the complete A.I.M. process. He did not lose his competitiveness and remained a very gregarious, engaging man. He did learn, through his voyage of self-discovery, to have a "Plan A and B" at every step as he moved forward. When he had the impulse to act before thinking, he learned to review his thinking process so he could determine the decisions that would move him towards his eventual goal. Barb's journey, meanwhile, allowed her to move with her husband while exploring the new career directions she had identified through the process. Through deep and very personal reflection and research, she was finally able to identify several areas that *she* wanted to pursue.

Your result: A foundation to move forward

At the end of this first, important stage of the A.I.M. process, you should have a simple statement that will focus your efforts as you move forward. You are now ready, through the next stage, to understand your past in more detail so you can prepare for your future.

Mapping the Four-Dimensional You

Have patience with all things, but chiefly have patience with yourself. Do not lose courage in considering your own imperfections but instantly set about remedying them. Every day, begin the task anew.

—Saint Francis de Sales

People, it seems, are caught in a struggle between looking back and looking forward. We often deride those who spend too much time thinking about the past. "He's yesterday's man," is a criticism often leveled in political circles. "What's done is done," we tell others, "Live for today."

Yet those of us who live thinking only of the future are also challenged. As a society, we embrace the new and quickly forget the old. Every day, we act and react to all that goes on around us, trying to complete the tasks we have set for ourselves. We go from home to work to home, juggling meetings or family or school obligations day after day. When we do think about anything, it is to think ahead, looking at what our next task is, or what we have scheduled for the next week.

When we take time off to lie on a beach or get away from the stresses of life, what do we do? We think further ahead. What do I want to do with the rest of my life? How can I better support my partner or my family in the years to come? What do I have to do to get to the next stage in my life?

While looking ahead and thinking of the changes you need to make is generally a good thing, we often do not find that balance between forward thought and realizing how we got where we are. What decisions did we make that brought us to this point in life? Were there things we could have done differently? And are there patterns that keep repeating themselves in our lives that influence where we go and how we might be stuck where we are?

This focus on the present and future often causes us to live narrow lives. Usually, we tend to focus most of our attention on one or two areas and define ourselves through them, considering what we are doing right now and what we will do in the weeks and months to come. We all know busy career professionals who spend most of their time thinking and talking about their work. Ditto the committed family person who always references his/her children and their accomplishments. But as we all know, there are many different dimensions to what makes a person unique. The busy career person may have been a poet or an artist in university. The committed parent may be active in their church, mosque or synagogue, but have an unrealized ambition that has nothing to do with their family or spiritual lives. The busy career person may have had a promising future as a poet or sculptor, but cut short their artistic endeavors to focus on what the rest of the world told them was important. The unfortunate thing about modern life is that we are often not conscious of the other dimensions of our lives or how we may keep these aspects hidden as we narrow our focus on what we think "really matters."

These issues will be the focus of this chapter. We will present exercises that will help you explore different dimensions of your personality. We will help you look back and review some of the things that have characterized your life so far. With this deeper knowledge of yourself, you can then look forward to proceed through the next stages of the A.I.M. process.

The windowpane exercise: Looking inside yourself—from the outside!

There are many ways people can perform self-analysis exercises. Surveys and studies can measure thousands of different variables about a person's character, outlook, and overall makeup. Human resources professionals, for example, will often use personality inventories, IQ tests, or other instruments to place people in categories that help others understand their motivations and better manage them.

The coaching profession has its own tools and instruments. Along with many of my fellow professionals in the field, I use a simple "windowpane" exercise at the start of my coaching engagement to better understand my clients. This exercise asks them to look at their lives through four "frames": professional, personal, physical, and spiritual. We all have basic needs and desires in each of these frames or quadrants, and understanding what is important to a client in these areas helps me explore what they value, what motivates them, and how the coaching process can be tailored to address their issues.

MAPPING THE FOUR-DIMENSIONAL YOU THROUGH THE WINDOWPANE EXERCISE: *Highlight what you value and what you can observe about yourself with respect to each of these four quadrants.*

Professional	Personal
Physical	**Spiritual**

Before we ask you to work through your own windowpane exercise, let's walk through the four quadrants using the example of Lorri, a vice president at a major bank whom I coached through a major transition.

The **professional quadrant** captures information about the evolution and highlights of someone's career in terms of positions held, organizations, attributes, etc. Lorri offered the following observations in this quadrant:

- I am the VP for marketing at a major bank;
- My entire career has been in marketing;
- I am rated as "high potential";
- I am known as a team player and empower others;
- I like what I do, but the industry is experiencing troubled times;
- Is this the time where I can maximize my potential in the bank?; and
- How can I stand out from the crowd or do I want to make a break into a different field with more potential?

The **personal quadrant** captures information about what is important with respect to your personal relationships with your partner or family, your political beliefs, your financial goals, etc. In Lorri's case, she offered the following observations:

- I am married with two children in elementary school;
- My husband works in the public sector;
- We own a house with a $300,000 mortgage;
- I earn $150,000 and have a good pension plan;
- We are soon going to take an ailing parent into the house;
- We are very conservative;
- Family takes up my time outside of work; and
- We love where we live and don't want to move.

The **physical quadrant** captures your observations about your health, fitness, or other elements related to your overall well-being.

In this quadrant, clients often reveal how their stress is manifesting itself or talk about their need for work/life balance. In Lorri's case, she offered the following observations:

- My health is good and I have regular checkups;
- I work out at the company gym a couple of times a week;
- I generally feel energetic, but after a few weeks of constant work I need to recharge; and
- Sometimes I worry if the constant stress between my work and life will suddenly result in a serious medical condition.

All human beings have a more introspective side that relates to emotional elements or those beyond immediate physical needs. These items are captured in the **spiritual quadrant**, where you can note your personal beliefs and values. It does not have to involve your specific religious orientation or faith in a higher power. In Lorri's case, she offered the following observations:

- I truly respect diversity;
- I believe that doing good deeds increases your odds for good opportunities;
- For me, my family is number one; and
- I want to feel, at the end of the day, that I have made people feel good about themselves and that I can sleep at night knowing that I am fulfilled.

Learning from George and Jessica

I began helping people map these four dimensions almost at the start of my coaching practice. Since that time, I have walked hundreds of professionals through its various points. As I think back about the results I have had with this exercise, two examples—those of George and Jessica—stand out.

I first met George when he was completing an intense year in a full-time MBA program. From his childhood spent in a small rural farming town, he had gone to university and taken a science degree, then begun a very successful career with a plastics manufacturing company. He had always felt, however, that his science background had limited his ability to move into higher management. So, after ten years of toiling in middle management, he enrolled in an intensive MBA program. George was fully committed to the program, deciding to take a year off work (without pay) and to relocate his family so they could all live near the university while he studied full time.

The MBA program he had chosen was ahead of many others at the time. As part of its comprehensive course offering, it made professional coaching available to its students to help their transition back to the workforce. Most of the students were high achievers whose ambition and sense of their own potential had become ever sharper through their studies, giving them very different aspirations once they finished their year in the program. Many, as it turned out, would not necessarily return to their original employer, and benefited from time spent with professional coaches who could help them shape their thoughts and consider their options.

Between my many international and domestic coaching assignments, I found some time to offer my services to the students in the program. So, by the luck of the draw, I became George's coach.

I first met George in the school's student lounge. The man who settled into the easy chair opposite me was in his mid-thirties, athletic, with graying brown hair, and wearing khakis and a polo shirt. Our easy banter quickly gave way to some focused discussion, as George began parrying my initial questions with pointed questions of his own about my relationship to the MBA program, my coaching process, and what he could expect from it. As our discussion progressed, however, he began to relax a little. He explained that his employer saw him as a "typical engineer" whose strong technical skills led him into the production side of the company. While George did not initially strike me as the type of person predisposed to talking about his feelings and having a strategic view of his career, he did surprise me with his observation that, if he kept on his current path, the best he could hope for would be a middle-management technical position or, in a best-case scenario, becoming vice president of manufacturing.

"I can do more than that, Jim," he explained. "I think that with the right training and perspective I can make a real difference in my career. I just need to find out how to get there."

With this perspective and interest in change, it was no surprise to me that George took to the windowpane exercise with real gusto. He spent the next several days adding details and considering the questions it posed. At our next meeting, we reviewed the material together. I asked a number of questions so we could both understand the points he had raised. At this stage in the process, most of a coach's questioning is simply for the purpose of clarity. You do not want to put any "buts" in the way of a deeper dialogue, as the analysis will come out later in the process.

In George's four-dimensional map of his priorities, one point stood out above all others. In the "personal" corner of his window, one of his bullet points read: "I want to be able to take my boys fishing after work." When I asked him about this, his eyes lit up and he became very passionate. He began talking about his rural roots and the importance of family, how he had gone fishing with his own father and still thought about those times. For George, it was immediately clear that no matter what he did in his career, he wanted to make sure that he made time to have that kind of experience with his own children so they too would have similar fond memories when they became adults.

The more we discussed this point, the more it became a deciding factor for George's future. He revealed during subsequent sessions that he was considering two very different job offers and had hoped that I could tell him what to do. I did not take the bait, but challenged him to reflect on what we had learned in the windowpane exercise. Without betraying what I thought, I asked him if anything stood out when he reviewed that material, in light of the decision that he now faced. It took some time, but eventually the light went on. He jabbed his finger at the personal quadrant and said, "Jim, I want to be able to take my boys fishing after work."

One of the offers he was considering clearly gave him the opportunity to fill that wish. While that prospective position paid less money than the other, it offered him the chance to relocate to a rural area. Moreover, it was with an entrepreneurial company that could give him flexible hours while committing to fast tracking George to becoming a general manager.

George decided to take this position a few months later. I am certain that if I were to visit his office on a Friday afternoon in the spring or summer, it would have a sign on the door that said, "gone fishing." And, if I were to wander down to the local river or lake, I could probably find him with his two boys, casting lines into the water, laughing as he builds memories for them that he values so much from his time with his own father.

Jessica's example is no less poignant. Her A.I.M. process led us to uncover a conflict between her spiritual/personal values and the achievements she had outlined in the professional side of her life.

Jessica was a respected partner in a large law firm who was referred to me by another coach. When we spoke briefly over the phone to find a time and place to meet, it was immediately clear that she was all about business. Our meeting the next day confirmed this. As I normally do, I arrived 10 minutes early for our appointment to find her already waiting in the coffee shop, checking her watch and making notations in her agenda.

Jessica was a slight woman in her early fifties, dressed in a conservative dark business suit, and giving me only the briefest of smiles as I introduced myself and sat opposite her. She immediately began asking questions about coaching, speaking at a very rapid pace while fidgeting with her pen and making occasional notes.

When I outlined the many distinct steps of my coaching process, it was clear from her face that she thought this would take too long to give her what she wanted. In fact, she suggested that we skip several of the initial stages, including the windowpane exercise, and move to what she thought was more important—helping her find a solution to her current challenge.

Politely, but firmly, I stuck to my guns. I explained that my approach was not an *à la carte* menu and that each step related to the next. I assured her that by the end of the process, we should be able to come to some conclusions that would help her with her challenges.

Still seeming a little unconvinced, she grudgingly agreed and began to tell me her story.

Jessica had made a fairly rapid rise to partner after joining her firm shortly after leaving law school. She was a technical expert on mergers and acquisitions, and regularly participated in multi-million dollar deals that spanned several different firms and countries. She admitted to me that she was frustrated with the other partners, feeling that they didn't listen to her and were often dismissive of her opinions.

"I'm almost always right, Jim," she said, "and they don't understand that they are hurting the firm and its clients if they don't adopt my recommendations."

Her friction with the other partners was becoming a problem. They had explained to her that, while they understood and valued her input, their final decisions often had to be made based on a variety of opinions and viewpoints. They could not simply rely on one person's viewpoint every time.

Jessica was dissatisfied with this explanation and found herself at a crossroads with the other partners about her future at the firm. One of the remedies suggested by her colleagues was that she engage a coach who could help her look at her career inside the firm, and also any options that might be available in the world outside its doors.

With this background in hand, I asked Jessica to complete the windowpane exercise. Reviewing the findings with her a few weeks later, I found much of its content fit nicely with what she had told me in the coffee shop. She had noted her quick ascent in the legal profession, the fact that she valued businesslike approaches, and her pride in her discipline and professionalism.

But certain points from various parts of her window stood out. In the spiritual quadrant, Jessica had made very strong statements about her confidence in her own abilities and unwillingness to compromise. She had said that, as the only expert in her field at the firm, she was 100 percent certain that her views in such matters were the only ones they should consider. She added that she had always had difficulties in compromising her values, and was certainly not willing to downplay or second-guess her contribution in this area in order to placate her partners.

Her musings in her personal quadrant were also interesting. She talked about a clear love of the outdoors and how she wanted to spend more time at the cottage to sail and golf. In her professional quadrant, she pointed out that she really enjoyed the legal profession and, if she had to leave her firm, she wanted to find another environment that would be more respectful of her expertise. She mentioned that she was willing to explore consulting, thinking that it might offer more flexibility while still allowing her to stay in her field. Lastly, she said she was willing to remain in her firm, but only if she could become more accepting of the limitations it presented.

This gave us a lot to work with in the subsequent stages of the coaching process. As I probed her values and aspirations in future discussions, she began to realize that staying in her current firm was not an option. Again and again she referred to her inflexibility around providing the right course of action that she had captured in the spiritual side of her window, stressing her commitment to provide the right answer, no matter what.

At this point, I offered some tough love. "Jessica," I said, "you realize that if you are not flexible at all, no one will want to work with you?"

To say she was taken aback was an understatement. After she mulled this over for a while, we explored this further. She slowly came to realize that the legal world was often built on a compromise between what was "right" and what clients were willing to accept. And it was these compromises—especially in her area of expertise—which she was increasingly unwilling to make.

As we talked about her options and reviewed her windowpane musings, I pointed to her love of the outdoors and the mention of the consulting option.

"Tell me more about this," I asked. "If you really value these things, is there a way for you to bring them together professionally?"

Jessica paused for a moment, and then her face lit up. The next hour of conversation flew by in a blur. She talked about the differences between the consulting and legal professions. We agreed that consulting might offer a way for her to avoid her need to always provide the right opinion, as consultants offer perspectives on the challenges facing their clients, it is up to the client to either accept or ignore the advice. This seemed to be an ideal way for Jessica to remain committed to her ideals of professionalism, while doing so in a professional environment. Consulting also opened up interesting opportunities for her to work virtually from her cottage.

This approach was appealing to Jessica, as she was well-known in her field for her expertise and the quality of her work. If she pursued consulting, then she could provide advice to a succession of clients and then move on to the next project. She could also spend a larger portion of her time working remotely from either her home or her cottage, thereby satisfying her personal interests. She also had the option of setting up her own practice or finding a home within a small group of like-minded professionals.

In the following months, Jessica did exactly that. She went on to set up her own firm and is now successfully self-employed. She is no longer troubled by the need to keep her peers happy. She works out of her cottage most of the time, finding time each week to sail or just enjoy the outdoors.

For both George and Jessica, the windowpane exercise was crucial to helping each of them understand the options that emerged later in the coaching process. Without it, they may have simply acted on instinct and reacted quickly to their challenges without thinking about *why* they were acting that way. As is the case with decisions we all make every day, both could have made what seemed like a "logical" decision that, in all probability, would have been at odds with their deeper personal needs. With each of them, finding out what they truly valued helped them to chart a new course that increased their chances of being truly happy.

Creating your own windowpane

Now I would like you to create your own windowpane.

On a sheet of paper or in a word processing file, sketch a four-part square like the one illustrated earlier in this chapter, and title each of the four quadrants—professional, personal, physical, and spiritual. In each, jot down quickly what you observe about yourself, just as Lorri, George, and Jessica did in the preceding stories. Don't spend too much time thinking about what and how you want to say things—just go with your first instincts. When you are done, close the file or store your sheet of paper and relax. We will come back to it later in the process.

Decade review: Looking back to move forward

Our next exercise explores how your past affects your future. The previous windowpane exercise was about the present, asking the question, "What do I know about myself right now?" The "decade review" exercise uses the same elements as the windowpane, but applies them to each decade of your life up to this point. Underlying this exercise is the idea that we can only understand why we are who we are by looking back at the major events that have shaped us up to this point.

The first time I completed this exercise for myself, I was skeptical. My first coach, Jim Bird, had asked me to do my own windowpane exercise and to review the major things that had happened to me in each decade of my life. I avoided completing both of these. "I know myself," the voice inside my head told me. "I don't need this self-awareness mumbo jumbo to tell me what I have to do."

Coach Bird, in each of our meetings, reinforced the necessity of completing both exercises. It wasn't until I was on a plane to the West Coast to visit my parents that I pulled out a legal note pad and began jotting down some ideas for each exercise. A slow start quickly turned into a torrent. When the plan landed five hours later, I was still writing!

My coach had asked me to take a pad of paper and write on the top of each sheet the decade in my life that it represented. He then told me to identify the most important events that had happened to me in each of those decades. For each event, I was to describe it and code it as one (or more) of the four dimensions in the windowpane exercise (professional, personal, physical, or spiritual). I was then supposed to describe why the event was significant and what was its impact on me.

Here are some of the events I identified for Coach Bird:

Decade: 1960s	
Event	When I was twelve, my parents took me off the bantam hockey team because I wasn't doing well in school.
Dimension	Personal.
Significance	It was the first time I felt intense shame and embarrassment in front of my friends; I felt that my parents and teacher were against me and that I was alone in the world.
Impact	I could have pouted or sulked, or I could take it on the chin, fight back, and return to the team at playoff time. I did fight back and learned how to rededicate myself to keeping up in school. I learned to respect my parents and the relationship between hard work and reward.

Decade: 1970s	
Event	My wife took a new job in Toronto, necessitating a re-location for me from Montreal; I hadn't been with my company long, and couldn't transfer for another year.
Dimension	Personal, professional, and physical.
Significance	We both suffered from upheaval on many fronts and learned how to deal with a long-distance relationship.
Impact	This caused a great deal of stress on our relationship; we learned that too much change on all fronts was a bad idea and we should never repeat it.

As the plane taxied towards the terminal and my waiting parents, I re-read the sheets I had written and began to see some patterns emerge in my past actions. When a big change happened in my life, I had often responded by panicking and changing many other, unrelated things in my life. Need to change jobs? Great, let's move to a new neighborhood at the same time. Changing roles at work? Fine, let's take up a new sport or buy a new car. I noted with my yellow highlighter that there were many more significant events in the categories other than professional. This told me that, perhaps, I had spent more time moving up the corporate ladder versus thinking about the other people in my life.

As I walked into the terminal and hugged my parents, I felt both unsettled and excited, as if a new world was opening to me. I was pumped and felt I could manage this new level of understanding. I even started to feel cocky—this could be something that could take my career to the next level.

Then, I sat in the car, and my father matter-of-factly said, "Well, Jim, your mother has Alzheimer's disease." My optimism, my cockiness, and my nicely rationalized sense of personal and professional space instantly disappeared.

We talked about it on the drive to their condo, with my mother trading very frank observations with my father from the back seat of the car as he drove. The diagnosis had come as an accident. My mother's eye doctor had noticed that she wasn't completing her sentences and asked her to talk with her physician, who—after a few tests—gave her the diagnosis.

We talked throughout the weekend about what this meant for them and what I could do, as their only child, to help them. Within six months of that day, I would hardly recognize my mother as her disease progressed rapidly. I watched my father, always a strong and focused man, grow older before my eyes as he helped her deal with the changes brought on by this devastating disease.

On the flight home, leafing through the handwritten sheets I had so optimistically filled out on my previous flight, I realized that the changes going on in my work life were nothing compared to other priorities that life imposes on you at random.

Back at my desk in the following weeks, I rearranged my schedule for the coming months to make sure I had time to visit my parents more frequently. I also picked up the phone and called Jim Bird to book our next session.

Years later, I still refer back to what I captured in both my windowpane exercise and my decade review. It helped me to understand where I was and how I had gotten there. That understanding, in turn, helped me assist my parents to deal with the devastating diagnosis and, almost incidentally, move my career forward. From that date onwards, I have never underestimated the power of perspective to help people assess their situation and then make new choices.

What you have accomplished

In this chapter, you should have completed the windowpane exercise that maps the "four-dimensional you," identifying a snapshot of what matters to you now in those four important quadrants. The decade review exercise should have provided you with a chronology of the important events in each decade of your life. Put both files away—we will come back to them as we move through the process.

CHAPTER 5

Sketching Success

Good plans shape good decisions. That's why good planning helps to make elusive dreams come true.

—Lester R. Bittel

In the previous chapter, we used two tools—the windowpane exercise and the decade review—to explore our values and the role that past events might play in motivating us to make decisions in the present.

Both of these tools allowed us to understand the foundations of our behavior and values. Our lives, like buildings, are built on foundations. And before you embark on renovations, you should understand the nature of the foundation the building was laid upon. Just as it is important to know and understand our historical base, we also must have a realistic understanding of our professional lives. If we are to progress to the final stages of the A.I.M. process and begin to move our lives in a new direction, we need to take stock of our skills, knowing our strengths, and more importantly—knowing where we might improve. Through some simple exercises, this chapter will help us understand how our current strengths and weaknesses relate to our ambitions, dreams, and visions for the future.

Knowing your skill/talent portfolio

In addition to my international coaching practice, I also work as an executive search consultant. In that role, I spend a lot of time on behalf of my clients interviewing candidates for a variety of executive positions. No matter who the client is or how senior the position, I always find time to ask every candidate the same question: "Tell me about your strengths and weaknesses."

Candidates, for the most part, hate this question. They think it is too basic and avoids the depth and breadth of their experience. "Why isn't he asking me about the last company I ran?" I can hear them thinking. I can also see them immediately begin to worry that they won't be able to give the perfect answer to the question. Their brows furrow or they stare at me for a moment, and I know they are thinking: "What does this guy want to hear from me?"

These reactions from candidates are predictable and underscore a simple truth. When anyone asks someone to "tell me about yourself," what they are really saying is, "Explain to me how well you know yourself—and how honest can you be about your strengths and weaknesses?"

The reactions I receive can tell me a lot about the candidates for an executive position. If the candidates don't know themselves, the answer is likely to come out muddled and uncertain. For example, I have people say things like, "I think I am a team player;" "I am a really motivated person;" "I am a self-starter;" "I empower people;" "I am not a very good politician, but I play the game;" and last, but not least, "I can't recall any obvious weaknesses."

You might ask what is wrong with these answers? If you look closely, most of them are open-ended. They give a smart interviewer a lot of room to dig further, finding out more and more about the candidates in ways that they might not choose to present themselves. For example:

- "You *think* you're a team player? Does that mean you haven't had positive feedback about your team skills?"
- "You aren't conscious of *any* weaknesses you might have? Would people you have worked with say the same thing about you?"

- "You play political *games* at your office? Doesn't that get in the way of what you should be doing?"

You get the picture. If you can't offer a realistic idea of what you do well and those things with which you might need help, how can you really present yourself to an interviewer without risking that you will make a bad case worse?

The exercises in this chapter help you prepare to give that answer. They serve as important ways to help you assess the options you have to move your career or life forward. Put simply, the more you know yourself, the easier it will be to determine which future opportunities are a good fit with the skills you already have.

Self-knowledge—a study in contrasts: The story of Caroline and Greg

To appreciate how important it is to know your own strengths and weaknesses, you need look no further than two examples from my practice—Caroline and Greg.

Caroline was a chief operating officer in a law firm whom I met during the search process for a position I was looking to fill for a client. David, a colleague of hers, had called me and recommended that I see her. I knew David quite well—well enough to know that he didn't readily recommend others, so I looked forward to my meeting with Caroline.

I wasn't disappointed. As she walked into my office, Caroline exuded confidence. In her early fifties, she was smartly tailored with an optimistic bearing and a firm handshake. The poise and excitement in her voice when she began talking about her career was tangible, and was refreshing coming from someone who held down one of the most difficult positions in a law firm. My experience with people who manage the administration at such firms is that they are often taken for granted by a stable of lawyers who too often focus more on their own billings, overlooking the administrative procedures and the staff who are necessary to make them work.

As she began to outline what had brought her to me, I immediately thought that she was already living the first two stages of the

A.I.M. process. She talked about her twenty years of experience with various professional services firms and her desire to explore other career options. She effortlessly moved on to talk about her life experience and personal values. She had grown up in a big mid-western city in the United States with great parents and two brothers. Her family had been active in outdoor sports, giving her memories of hiking and camping that she carried with her to this day. Consequently, she explained, she always made time for family and valued the fact that the firms she had worked for embraced a work/life balance. Caroline, without knowing it, had conducted her own windowpane exercise in all but name, and was quite familiar with the events and values that continued to shape her life thus far.

My appreciation of her level of self-awareness only grew when she moved on to talk about her strengths and weaknesses. In response to my standard question, she settled into the chair in my office, furrowed her brow, and thought for just a minute.

"I know I am strong in the following skills, Jim, because I've heard about them from my superiors, colleagues, staff, and friends." She then went on to outline the following:

- I have excellent skills in reporting and analyzing financial data. I have created numerous annual budgets that were demanding and complex, but I always get them done on time and they are very well received.
- My staff says I make them think and I encourage debate. I value and want input from others.
- I enjoy leading teams. I think this is because I was mentored very well by a succession of great bosses. I learned from them to respect that every staff member is critical to your success.
- I was initially afraid of technology, but I have learned all that I need to know. I now enjoy using it and it makes my life easier.

When it came to weaknesses, she again paused for only a moment, leaned forward in her chair before outlining the following:

- I am not a very good politician in the workplace. Going forward in my life, I need to be mindful of that fact and hope I can be in an environment where this is not a major requirement.
- I am used to working with well-educated people who think about their work and bring a really informed perspective to it. I wouldn't do well in an environment that didn't value education or foresight.
- Sometimes, people see me as "bookish." It must be my accounting background. So, I could use a little help in becoming more open and relaxed around others.

Hearing this as I sat across from Caroline, I was struck by how honest her assessment was, and how much it resonated with what I could see in her mannerisms and attitude. The fact that she knew herself so well, and was confident enough to share that with someone who had the ability to recommend her—or not recommend her—for potential new positions, was very impressive. As our conversation progressed, I found myself offering to help Caroline with her job search by connecting her to others in my network, as I was sure that they would see the same thing I had—a confident professional with a realistic opinion of her strengths and weaknesses. Because of this, she would be an asset to any workplace.

I couldn't help but contrast my experience with Caroline to one I had only a few weeks later with Greg. While Caroline's inherent self-knowledge and realistic perspective were obvious assets, Greg was her polar opposite.

I saw Greg on the recommendation of Raj, one of my former coaching clients. He had contacted me to ask whether I would be able to coach a colleague of his who was facing some career and life choices, but didn't seem to know where to turn. I agreed, and after a few calls and e-mails, Greg sat opposite my desk in the same chair that Caroline had occupied just weeks earlier.

In his late thirties, Greg looked a lot like a film star, with wavy hair and a smooth, yet animated, face. Like Caroline, he was an excellent communicator. He was warm, upbeat, and concise in describing the basic facts of his life. In our initial conversation, he shared that he had grown up in a small town, had been a gifted athlete early in life, and was now happily married with two children. He had risen to become a partner and minority shareholder in a medium-sized consulting firm.

I enjoy meeting happy and satisfied people. In my experience, many of these people actually underestimate their potential. While that inherent modesty often contributes to their success, it can also serve to hold them back at critical junctures in their career and life, and that was certainly the case with Greg.

After moving through the initial pleasantries, Greg explained that he was facing an immediate challenge with his work. His firm was about to be taken over by a larger company. Greg had been with the firm for a few years and quite enjoyed his job. Consequently, he feared that because he was unknown by the new management of the company, he might be fired or shunted to the side and given an uninteresting position. He realized he needed to take the initiative in meeting with the new management to carve out a good place for himself in the new company; otherwise, his life could become very difficult over the next few years.

"Jim," he asked, "how can I get on the radar with these guys and make sure I manage this opportunity properly? The new CEO will be running the show and I want to make sure he understands what I can do for the firm."

I thought for a moment before replying. Then I came back with a variant of my classic question.

"Greg, what will you say when the new CEO asks, 'So tell me about yourself?'"

Greg's eyes narrowed. He looked at me, looked away, and looked back again. It appeared that the most basic question I could ask had flummoxed him. Then he did what so many candidates I interview for executive positions do—he tried to tell me what he thought I wanted to hear.

His answer was a jumble of conditional responses, open-ended statements, and noncommittal generalities: "I guess others would say that I . . ." and "I'm a people person . . ." and "I believe in peak performance . . . ."

I listened, asking Greg more and more questions for clarification before letting his meandering explanations peter out on their own accord. Without having to say a word to him, a look of realization began to dawn on his face.

"Jim," he said, "I really have to do some work on that. If I don't know myself, how can I expect to explain myself to the new CEO?"

In the next few weeks, I worked Greg through a variety of exercises, finally coming to the strengths and weakness exercise explained in this chapter. With it, Greg generated the following list:

Strengths:

- I have spent my entire career to date with the same firm, progressing from the consultant level to executive in ten years. I enjoy my firm very much and I value that they have been very supportive of my efforts to advance my education.
- I like working in a team. I was an all-star in college football, and appreciated that you can't win without having the support of your teammates. I have applied this principle in my work, although my team at work sees that I am driven to win, but not at all costs. Many on my team have gone on to join the partnership, and some have left the firm, but on good terms and with positive memories of their experience with me.

Weaknesses:

- I don't have a lot of tolerance for people who whine and complain. In my world "the cup is half full;" therefore, I have to try harder to listen to people who may be very capable with good ideas, but who don't have the same optimism I have.
- I know that I have an entrepreneurial instinct, inherited from my father who never worked for anyone. However, there are all kinds of people in the workplace who are not self-starters, but can make a good contribution—I have to learn to better manage those people.

With these points in hand, Greg was ready for the meeting with his new CEO. Having prepared himself to make his case, his original 30-minute meeting with his new boss ran over an hour and a half. During the meeting, the CEO asked very detailed questions about Greg's education and, after discussing his strengths and weaknesses, he even went on to talk about his need to find a successor in the organization. Greg's preparation had paid off, putting him in a much better position with his new boss than he had hoped for.

Conducting your own exercise

It is now time for you to make your own realistic strengths and weaknesses list. Take a blank sheet of paper and divide it into half, or set up two columns on your computer screen, with strengths on one side, weaknesses on the other. As was the case with earlier exercises, don't think too much about what you are writing at first. Quickly get down everything you can think of on either side. Don't hold back, and don't second-guess yourself—just get it down on paper!

To get you started and give you an example, here is my own list of strengths and weaknesses.

Strengths	Weaknesses
I am a sociable and friendly person.	I am not patient with detail and rely on others to help me deal with that.
I am a good facilitator—I can put people at ease and help them talk with one another.	
	I am easily frustrated by bureaucracy or processes that are done simply for the sake of process.
I am a lateral thinker who generates ideas that get people thinking differently.	
I am an optimist who generally sees the good in people and situations—I am always ready to help out.	When a major change happens in my life, my natural response is to try to change other things at the same time, usually making my problem worse.
I read people fairly well.	Technology is a bit of a barrier for me—sometimes I see it as gadgetry that unnecessarily complicates my life.

Go ahead and complete your own list. Once you have written down everything you can think of, go over it once to edit and polish it, ensuring you are comfortable with what you are saying about yourself. Be sure you are being as honest as possible—honesty is the starting point for this process.

With your list completed, put it aside with your other materials. We will return to it later.

Making a "future options" list of what you want in your career and/or life

This part of the A.I.M. process is one of my favorites, coming just when clients have done some tough sledding and are wondering what to do. The previous exercises often leave people twisted into knots. They have been asked to look deep within themselves and face what could be some unpleasant truths. Many of my clients become restive and anxious at this stage, asking "When will this be over?" or they say, "I'm tired of all this process."

It is completely natural for human beings to want to get to the "fun stuff." Delayed gratification is certainly not a strength for most people, and when people want to make major changes in their lives, they often just want to get on with it.

Be patient. The following exercise will neatly complement those that you have already done. In the past few exercises, you have looked at what shapes your decision-making process, what you value, as well as reviewed your strengths and weaknesses. Now it is time for you to determine where you want to go in the future.

Sound simple? Well, not really. There is a reason why A.I.M. has a stage where you determine what goals you want to set in your career or life. Think for a moment about the incredible diversity of choices that any one person can make or the number of choices you have made to end up where you are. I would wager that most of those choices were not "choices" at all. Most of us did not out-line what we wanted when we were looking for our first job or chose whom to marry or what school to attend. Most of us end up just "going with the flow" to some extent or another. Certainly we do think about what we want in a job—level of compensation, type of work, etc.—but few of us systematically think through all of our options before deciding on the one we think is the best one for us.

The same could be said about the life partner we choose. Even though Internet dating has made choosing a partner a little more scientific in recent years, few of us can say that we used a rigorous process to identify what we liked, and did not like, in a partner before we decided to settle into a relationship.

So, at this point in the A.I.M. process, you are going to take the time to outline possible directions that you want to explore. The work you have done to this point to identify who you are and what you value will give you an excellent starting point to develop a checklist of areas you would like to explore as you move forward.

If you were designing a dream home from scratch, you would begin by establishing specific and reasonable criteria for what the house should look like, including working with an architect to develop detailed plans. At the end of the day, you would probably have a dream home that met all of your criteria. If you were buying a car, wouldn't you read a few reviews, conduct a bit of research, ask your friends for recommendations, and *then* make a decision? Sure you would. And deciding on a new direction in life should be accorded the same level of thought and consideration.

This is why creating a future options list is important. This exercise will help you identify a variety of areas that you can explore which, hopefully, will match nicely with what you have already outlined in the exercises that have led up to this point.

CEO or bus driver?: Paul's story

Helping someone map their options in life can lead a person in strange and interesting directions. A few years ago, I was coaching Paul, a CEO who worked in the hospitality industry. He was due to retire in five years, and his firm had suggested that he receive coaching well in advance of the transition. An active and engaging man in his late fifties, Paul knew that he would not be retiring to the golf course or to putter around in his garden, so he wanted to explore his options for other directions to take in his career/life.

Paul and I had several meetings to determine his sense of purpose going forward. We completed his windowpane exercise and reviewed his strengths and weaknesses list. When we reached the future options list exercise, however, his first few statements were as far apart from each other as I have ever seen.

Paul took a sheet of paper and divided it into several columns. He filled the first three with the following options:

1. I have always wanted to drive a bus.
2. I have run many marathons in my life and still have to run in Hawaii and Sydney.
3. My wife and I definitely want to do some volunteer work.

The fact that he could immediately name such varied possible areas he wanted to explore was very encouraging. Many of my clients balk when asked to take a clean page and turn it into a list of things they would like to explore as new directions in their lives. Many default to safer ground, talking about areas in which they have already worked, types of jobs they have previously held, or cities where they have already lived. Others are willing to venture a few ideas that could be called "outside the box," but then they immediately begin naming reasons why those ideas won't work for them.

This is why I liked Paul right away. He began his list with something so personal and so outside the box that I knew he was in the right frame of mind to brainstorm about new directions to take in his life. By saying he wanted to drive a bus, he showed that he was open to new ideas and to exploring things that would definitely be considered nontraditional.

I took the time to explore some additional ideas with Paul, and gradually a few serious options began to take shape that moved beyond his initial talk of becoming a bus driver. He shared with me that he had always wanted to teach. He was currently teaching part time in the hospitality industry, which he really enjoyed, and he thought that he might be able to do that full time.

He then added another column, which he titled "Not for profit." Under this category, he wrote about how he might want to work for various health causes, such as cancer, heart disease, and diabetes.

His last column was titled "management consulting." He was a highly respected expert in the hospitality industry, and thought it might be fun to travel the world and work on projects with hotels and private clubs.

From his outside-the-box start, Paul had identified several areas that he thought were worth further exploration. He had gone from a blank page and a question, to a number of potential opportunities to explore.

The second part of the exercise helped Paul narrow the field a little further. For each of the columns he had identified, he then added a separate list titled "ideal role/function/position."

Paul had been a CEO for more than twenty years and had no burning desire to perform that role again. Based on what he had learned in his strengths and weaknesses exercise, he knew that he enjoyed working in an advisory capacity just as much as he enjoyed running things. For the right opportunity, he would still be interested in being a senior manager, but not at the same pace as he had done as a CEO. Drawing on this knowledge, he identified that he could work in the roles of teacher, consultant, and/or general manager.

With the work he had already completed on his windowpane, strengths and weaknesses list, and future options list, we now had the basis to move forward. Paul felt good at this point because he now had a starter list of ideas to explore. As he continued to move through the process, he was confident that in the five years he had before retirement, he had enough information to explore his options.

Developing your own future options list

It is now time for you to develop your own future options list. Take a deep breath and don't be intimidated. The task here is to capture, either on paper or on a computer screen, directions you might want to explore as you move forward to change your career or life. There are no right or wrong answers. No one will judge what you write, so don't rein yourself in by thinking, "Well, that doesn't make sense" or "Oh, that just sounds silly." When you go with your own instincts, there is no telling how long or short the list will be, and it doesn't matter. This is *your* life and you are not comparing yourself to anyone else.

Divide a plain sheet of paper or a page on your computer into several blank columns that run from left to right across the page (on your computer, it might be a good idea to arrange your document in landscape format so you can fit more columns across the page from left to right). At the very top of the page, title the document "New directions I would like to explore in my career/life." Then, off the top of your head, begin writing ideas at the top of each column.

New directions I would like to explore in my career/life							
Ideal role							

Some people take to this exercise right away, writing page after page of ideas. Others are a little more hesitant, often struggling to find one or two areas they would like to explore. If you are uncomfortable doing this on your own, here are some tips that can help get you going:

- Do not allow yourself to second-guess what you are thinking. If a thought pops into your head, write it down.
- You may want to start with something that you already enjoy and want to build on. In Paul's case, he started with something he had thought about since childhood (I always wanted to drive a bus).
- You may want to review your windowpane exercise and/or the decade review before starting. Either of these exercises may offer clues to get you started.

Once you have captured all of the ideas you are able to, place a horizontal line that runs across the bottom of all columns. On the left margin, add a title called "Ideal role." Then, for each of the areas you have identified, brainstorm about what type of position you might have with respect to each idea. If you have identified a new company or type of industry you would like to work for, would you like to be a vice president or a manager? If you have identified that you want to explore a new sport, do you want to play it in a recreational league or competitively? If you have said you want to start a family, what is your ideal role with respect to that family? Do you want to evoke the examples set by your own parents or are you keen to explore new ground?

I found it hard to get started with this exercise when I did it for the first time. To get my thoughts moving, I re-read both my windowpane and decade review. In each of them, I saw that I had talked a lot about how much I valued independence, so immediately I added "owning my own business" to my future options list. I also noticed that I talked a lot about helping people and the enjoyment I got when others succeeded thanks to my help. This point led me to add "explore executive coaching" to my list.

Take your time. Capture everything you can and then put it to the side. We will revisit this exercise in the coming chapters as we begin to explore these new directions.

When it all comes together: Marilyn's story

I will leave you with a final story that illustrates the type of profound change that people can make in their lives when all of these exercises work together.

Marilyn was a sales executive in her early forties who worked in the food business. By all external standards, she was doing well. She had been frequently promoted, was well regarded by her colleagues, and had a rewarding family life. However, Marilyn was concerned that she had only worked for one large corporation for her entire working life. She knew no other world beyond its doors and she was beginning to think that there might be other challenges out there that could allow her to grow in new and different ways.

Marilyn's windowpane was one of the most balanced I have ever seen, with work success matched evenly by personal and family success. Her strengths and weaknesses list was very honest and forthright, and included the following:

Strengths:

- My early sports experience in basketball gave me a competitive spirit, but not at all costs.
- I was never the star player, but I played hard and was dedicated to doing my best.
- I like public speaking and feel comfortable meeting people at all levels and from a variety of backgrounds.
- My dad was in sales and I saw how happy he was. Every day was a new day to him, with lots of opportunity. This rubbed off on me.
- When I make commitments, I follow through on them.

Weaknesses:

- I am trusting to a fault, meaning I get really disappointed when others don't deliver on their promises to the team or to me.
- I think I naively trust that the company will always take care of me if I am doing my part—and that is dangerous. I could easily be sideswiped by a downturn or restructuring.
- My professional support network is totally within the company, and I haven't spent any time extending it into the wider world.

When we moved into the future options list, however, Marilyn ran into difficulty. She had no idea where, or how, to start. Even though she was committed to exploring her future and breezed through the early exercises in the A.I.M. process, the blank sheet that was to be used to list the areas she wanted to explore seemed to stymie her.

I eased Marilyn into the process by having her reflect on the exercises to date, and asked her to pick a really happy time in her life. Marilyn went back to her college experience with her basketball team, and noted how it had instilled in her a life-long love of sports. The more she talked about her sporting life, the more animated and engaged she became. I then asked her one question that tipped her into an entirely new way of thinking.

"Marilyn, if you could combine your experience and passion in sports with your work life, how would you feel?"

Her eyes immediately lit up. "That would be amazing, Jim!" She was about to add a "but" until I interrupted her.

"That's fine," I said, "write that down and let's explore it further."

She now had her first column titled "Sports/business" combination. From that initial start, the ideas then came fast and furiously. She began thinking about running her own business (in a column titled "Entrepreneurial situations") or working for a company that specialized in sporting goods. Other ideas followed on their heels, and, in the end, she had a comprehensive set of areas to explore that neatly complemented her earlier work on what she valued. As was the case with Paul, we now had options where initially there were none.

When she moved on to the "Ideal role" portion of the exercise, that part came to her more easily. Like her father, she was passionate about sales and was very happy to continue in that area, so she suggested sales-related roles for all of the ideas she had captured. The list, for now, was done.

You have identified your dreams

In both of these cases, Paul and Marilyn had a coach to guide them, but the basics of the method can be completed by anyone. One of the prime benefits of the exercises we have performed in this chapter is that they allow everyone to capture and explore their dreams. With this completed exercise in hand, it is now time to move forward and begin to put your newfound perspective into action.

CHAPTER 6

Reviewing What's Important

There are pauses amidst study, and even pauses of seeming idleness, in which a process goes on which may be likened to the digestion of food. In those seasons of repose, the powers are gathering their strength for new efforts.

—J.W. Alexander

Human beings are creatures of stories. In the early days of our existence, we gathered around campfires in the evenings to relive the stories of the day's hunt and hear the sagas of those who had come before us. We have always used stories to learn, to connect us with each other, and as reference points as we move in new directions. In simple terms, stories tell us where someone started, the challenges they faced, and how they overcame them. Good stories are sequential, logical, and instructive. They are told in a way that allows us to take away our own lessons and apply them to our lives.

Over the past few chapters, while you may not have been conscious of it, you have been writing your own story. We have moved from abstract thoughts about your situation in life (What is the challenge that I am facing? Why am I unhappy right now?), to focused introspection (What have been the highlights in the various decades of my life?), to honest discussion about what you do well and what you do not (What are my strengths and weaknesses?), to more concrete brainstorming about directions you might like to explore (What are some options for me?).

The exercises you have completed to answer these questions have taken what might have seemed to be a jumble of conflicting emotions, stresses, and feelings, and turned them into the beginnings of a story. This story should take things you may have thought were random and unconnected in the past, and begin to weave them into something bigger—a narrative where elements influence each other in ways you may have not thought possible before.

Our goal in this chapter is to review the exercises you have completed so far, turning them into a story that you understand and to which you can refer as you move into later stages in the A.I.M. process. What you learn about yourself in this review should allow you, for example, to make the best use of the networking calls we will make later in the process. What you learn should also increase the chances that the decisions you make will be a logical fit with your story to date, allowing you to write the next chapters in the story of your life.

From many options, a new direction: Henry's story

From all of the executives I have coached, Henry's story stands out as the perfect example of how this stage of the process helped him to kick his thinking into high gear, allowing him to move quickly to address the issues he was facing.

Henry and I were introduced by a friend of his, a lawyer whom I knew quite well. Facing a serious life choice, Henry had turned to his friend for advice. Immediately appreciating the magnitude of the opportunities facing Henry, his friend suggested that he should talk with someone who could give him professional advice and perspective on the challenge he was facing.

After a few phone calls and e-mails, Henry settled into the chair in my office and began to share with me the decisions that he now faced. Henry was a thirty-eight-year-old engineer who had risen quickly in the ranks of a multinational company. Since joining the firm straight out of university, Henry had been promoted every eighteen months and currently occupied a senior management position. Along the way, he had married his university sweetheart and had two young children.

"Until a few months ago, Jim, I thought things were fine," Henry confided, leaning towards me and running his hands through his hair. "And when my boss offered me a transfer to head office, I thought it was a great idea and took it."

Henry's new job was director of strategic planning for the company. In this position, his boss hoped he would learn new skills, such as interpreting financial data, and connect with senior executives from all aspects of the business. At first glance, it seemed to be a perfect springboard for Henry to move into a more senior executive position with the company he loved.

Soon after taking this position, however, Henry began to gain a new perspective about his firm. Its financials were not as solid as he had been led to believe. Some of the other executives were not as competent as he had thought. Competition from other firms was becoming far more fierce, and he wondered if his firm would be able to maintain its market position. He quickly determined that one of the best things he could recommend, as director of strategic planning, was that the firm should allow itself to be taken over by a rival. How could he break this news to his boss and the management team that had supported his rise through the company?

At the same time that he was grappling with this new appreciation of the company and its prospects, he had received a call from a headhunter. His rise within the company had not gone unnoticed in the broader industry, and a smaller, more entrepreneurial company was looking to hire him as its new general manager. Though smaller than his current firm, its market share was strong and growing, and its CEO was well respected as a visionary business leader. To add even more pressure to the equation, the new company wanted to move quickly and had asked Henry for an answer within two weeks.

This, in a nutshell, was what had brought Henry to my office.

"Jim," he sighed, "there is so much opportunity right now that I can't get my mind around it. How do I make the decision that is best for me and my family?"

I assured Henry we would do what we could together, to help him put the decisions he had to make in the appropriate context; a context which would help increase the chances that he would make a decision that he would be comfortable with and would have the greatest chance of success.

During the following week, we quickly worked through the initial stages of A.I.M. In a relatively short amount of time, we were standing in my office with the key elements of Henry's exercises spread out in front of us on a conference table.

Henry's focus statement:

> *I am at a crossroads in my career. My company has given me great opportunities to advance; however, there is a good chance the company may be sold. My entire career to date has been with this company. From time to time, I have wondered what it would be like to work in a smaller, entrepreneurial organization.*
>
> *I have recently been offered a position that would be very interesting. Considering the circumstances, I think this is a good time to look at all of my career options in a structured manner.*

Henry's windowpane exercise:

Professional:	*Personal:*
• I have spent fifteen successful years in a multinational company.	• I am happily married with two kids in primary school.
• I have strong operations and planning skills.	• We own our own home (with a $150,000 mortgage).
• I want to be a general manager in a company in this field.	• I am the sole wage earner with a low six-figure package.
• I wonder whether I would do better in a smaller, entrepreneurial company.	• We like the town in which we live, have lots of friends, and are very active in the community.
• My company may be sold and that would throw a wrench into my career.	• I am generally not a risk taker.
• Headhunters say I am very marketable.	

Physical:	Spiritual:
• I work out regularly, eat well, and generally maintain good health.	• I am very loyal to my company and my staff.
• I play hockey once a week with the guys.	• I am a team player and seek lots of input from my staff.
• We ski and do other outdoor sports as a family.	• Giving back to my community through my church and charities is important to me.
	• I am very trusting and trustworthy.
	• Work-life balance is vital to me.

Henry's strengths and weaknesses:

Strengths	Weaknesses
• A team player.	• To date, I haven't spent any time in marketing/sales, although I work with people in these functions all the time.
• Loyal and trusting.	
• Career has moved rapidly with promotions every eighteen months.	
• Very experienced in general operations and planning.	• The only working world I know is inside my existing company.
• Industrial products is the market space that I know best.	• My external network is weak.
• I am good at multi-tasking. Many of my positions in the company have required me to juggle many balls at one time.	• Because I am trusting, I tend to take people at face value too quickly.

Henry's future list:

	Staying where I am?	Another big company?	Smaller, entrepreneurial company?	Join a consulting practice?
	Stick it out and take my chances, since I have been treated well, there is no reason to think my successful career path should not continue.	The head-hunters tell me I am in demand, so maybe there is another big company out there that might give me more freedom.	I am intrigued about this possibility, as I have seen friends who have made this kind of move, and they seem to feel fulfilled and their ideas are being appreciated.	With my experience in operations and planning, is this the time to go into consulting and enhance my skills even more, probably with a large consulting shop that houses "best practices in my field?"
Ideal role	Current position	Similar to current position	Unknown	Unknown

As Henry and I reviewed the sheets spread out before us on the conference room table, it was obvious that his life, so far, was evolving as a compelling story. It was also apparent that he was facing a big fork in the road that would determine what his future career direction looked like.

Henry was a person with proven potential. He had moved through a succession of positions to a point where he was ready to make a significant move in his career. The other parts of his life were in balance, with his family and personal life supporting his achievements. His new position had allowed him to learn more about his firm than the rest of the executive team and, consequently, he was poised to play an important role in its future, should he choose to do so. His hard work had not gone unnoticed outside of his firm, and his reputation had now led to another option—joining a more entrepreneurial firm where he might make a greater impact than he had with his current firm. He also had the option, should he choose to explore it, of striking out on his own—something he had not even considered before he began mapping out his various options.

Even moving rapidly through the process allowed Henry to explore, with me, his options in more detail in the context of the story of his life to this point. Let's look at the options we explored and what Henry ultimately decided, given what the A.I.M. process helped him to see about his life.

"Staying where I am"

As Henry and I reviewed this option, he kept referring back to his windowpane exercise and what he had learned about his strengths and weaknesses. From his musings in the professional quadrant of his windowpane, he knew that he was well regarded by his colleagues within his company and he had done well by them in the past several years. His personal quadrant was also important, because if he chose this option, nothing would change at home. This was also the case with both the physical and spiritual quadrants, since staying in his current position would not challenge his values. However, the possibility of the company being sold created considerable risk that could impact all quadrants. Perhaps his colleagues would not be open to the option of selling the firm to a rival and they might blame him for raising the issue. If the sale did go ahead, there was no guarantee that the buyer would want him to stay with the firm or see his potential in the same light as his current co-workers.

When assessing what he might do to explore this option further, Henry realized that while he was well regarded for his capabilities and his loyalty, he ran the risk of being "run over" if he simply sat back and let others determine the future of the company. While he was happy at his current firm and his colleagues had never disappointed him, Henry had to ask himself what he could do to minimize the risk that the company could change abruptly and leave him behind.

To move forward with respect to this option, Henry drew up a list of those people he knew the best in the company—those he could trust to ask about the future of the firm, how a takeover might be received, and what his place might be in the new company. He would then approach those people, in confidence, to seek their counsel.

"Another big company"

Henry and I then reviewed another option—finding another large company in the same field and shifting his career ambitions in that direction. There were obvious pros and cons to this approach. Henry had built a solid career in his industry and had risen quickly to the top ranks of an established company. He had also, however, only worked for that one firm in the industry, so his knowledge was limited to how that company was structured and how it approached its market. While headhunters had recently begun approaching him and told him he would be in demand, were his skills and knowledge really that transferrable to another firm, and would they value his contributions in the same way that his current firm obviously had?

As we discussed this option, several other questions naturally emerged. Would moving to another large company in the same field just give him more of the same? Wouldn't it be better to take advantage of the need to make a change and make a significant one instead of a small one?

When we reflected on his windowpane exercise, I noted that he had identified that he wanted to be a general manager with a firm in his field. I asked him a basic question: "What do you think shifting to another large firm means for your desire to become a general manager?"

Henry thought about it for a minute, and then began to slowly nod his head.

"It could go two ways, Jim," he said. "I could be the new guy who comes in like a breath of fresh air and rises to the top quickly. Or, I could be the new guy who hasn't built the relationships and performance history necessary to be trusted with the top job."

These were valid points with no immediate answers. In order to move forward with respect to this option, we decided to turn the tables on the headhunters who had been calling Henry. He had developed a rapport with one of them, so he decided to sit down with her and get her perspective on the market, find out which firms might be interested in his qualifications, and what he might expect in terms of position and remuneration, etc.

"Smaller and more entrepreneurial company in my field"
As we discussed this third option, it became clear that Henry was very intrigued by the possibility of working in a more entrepreneurial environment. The recent call from a headhunter to discuss an opportunity at a smaller, more dynamic firm had opened up a new direction that Henry had not previously considered. He had also seen a close friend make a similar transition to a smaller firm and benefit enormously from the process.

Henry was also frank about the number of questions this option raised for him. We reviewed his windowpane exercise and revisited his stated aversion to taking risks. We discussed the fact that he was the sole earner for his family, who relied on his income to allow his wife to stay at home with their young children. We also explored his need for work-life balance, noting that in a smaller, more dynamic company there are often unexpected demands that cut into family and leisure time, often making the maintenance of boundaries much more difficult. Lastly, he pointed to the page upon which he had written about the weakness of his external network.

"Jim," he said, "if I am going to work in a more entrepreneurial environment, I will probably need a lot more contacts outside the company in order to help me succeed. That may be something I have to work on."

After considerable discussion, we mapped out a few steps to help Henry explore this option further. Since this option had emerged because a headhunter had called to discuss a possible job opportunity, Henry decided to follow this up and discuss where it might lead. He agreed to do so, however, recognizing that there were considerable risks with respect to this opportunity, so he was determined to approach it as potentially the first of many such opportunities and not one that had to be pursued at all costs. At the same time, he decided to meet with his friend who had made a similar career transition to discuss the pros and cons with him, seeking any advice he might offer.

"Join a consulting practice"
Henry's last option was one that emerged fairly late in our discussions. While most of our exploration had focused working for

variants of his current firm, some of the elements that emerged in his windowpane and other exercises pointed to another option. When we discussed his intimate knowledge of his industry, his commitment to teamwork, and the strong value he placed on work-life balance, he laughingly said, "Well, Jim, I could always be a consultant to firms just like mine."

But what had started as a jest quickly became an option that Henry was willing to consider. The idea of working in an environment where he could explore "promising practices" in his field and share them with other firms was very appealing to him. The idea of setting his own schedule and working as part of a consulting team also intrigued him, but he readily confessed that he knew little about the consulting world. Some of his former colleagues had moved into the field and prospered, while others had complained about the need for travel and the continual ups and downs of project-based work.

"On the surface, it seems like it might be a fit," Henry shared, "but I would have to do some more work here to determine if it is really a fit for me."

The consulting option presented the biggest unknown to Henry, and potentially the greatest departure from the story he had been building. His career, to date, had been about quickly moving up the corporate ladder towards a position as general manager. Transitioning to consulting would be a new path that could see him placing personal reward and independence above the corporate hierarchy in which he had been climbing so diligently these past several years.

In order to explore this path further, Henry decided to meet with several former colleagues who had made the transition to the consulting world to see if it would be a fit for him. In doing so, he also committed to refer back to the various A.I.M. exercises he had completed, to determine if the consulting life would be compatible with what he had learned about his own values and beliefs.

Henry's journey—from confusion to a story with choices

Within the short time that Henry and I worked together, he had made remarkable progress. The first few stages of the A.I.M. process had allowed him to move into a much better position to consider his options and explore them further. Initially, he had come into my office as a man who was conflicted by what seemed like an either/or choice between some very different options. Should he stay with his current company and risk becoming the champion of a takeover that might leave him out in the cold? Should he make an uncertain jump to another, smaller company that played by different rules? This was the choice that had faced Henry, but by going through the first few steps of the A.I.M. process, we had arrived at a much different appreciation of Henry's position.

He now realized that the challenges he faced were really opportunities. Rather than choosing between two very different options, Henry now appreciated that he had several other choices that made sense within the ongoing story of his career and life. Moreover, the exercises had put him on a path that had to explore these options, and definite reference points he could use as new opportunities presented themselves. This was a huge contrast to the either/or choice that had confronted him just a week before.

Henry now had a story that allowed him to place the choices he faced in a broader context. He had widened his options and could now consider them in light of a deeper understanding of his history, his motivations, and his values. He also had an initial path forward to explore these options in the coming months and years, putting him on the way to taking charge of his career and life. Moreover, he could now answer basic questions about where he was going, why he was going in that direction, and what he might do if new options presented themselves.

This was the beginning of Henry's story—a story that would continue by the choices that he made now and in the years to come. That story came from the first few exercises in the A.I.M. process— and we will pick it up in later chapters of this book.

Moving forward with your own story

Just as Henry crafted his own story from the understanding he gained from the initial A.I.M. exercises, it is now time for you to move forward with your own story. Specifically, it is time now to lay out exactly what you have learned about yourself, and consider what it is telling you. Once you are comfortable with the story it tells, you can then move on to the next stage of the A.I.M. process, where you share this story with others to gain a "reality check" on where you might be going.

Your first step is to spread out, on a table in front of you, the A.I.M. exercises you have completed so far. If all of your material is in electronic format, print the documents off in hard copy. You should have the following in front of you:

1. **Your focus statement:** This is your sentence or paragraph that clearly states the issue(s) you are facing and outlines your commitment to move forward with respect to it/ them.
2. **Four-dimensional you:** Your completed windowpane exercise that outlines what is important to you in each of the four quadrants of your life.
3. **Decade review:** Your completed series of significant events in each decade of your life.
4. **Sketching success:** Your list, compiled honestly, of your strengths and weakness.
5. **Future options list:** Your column-by-column list of areas you might like to explore in the future as you move forward.

These five pieces begin to tell a story about your life. The first three exercises outline what you are facing, what you value, and what important things have shaped your life and character over the course of your life. Steps four and five are where you begin to honestly appraise your current situation and brainstorm about your future. Taken together, they form something that few people have ever considered about themselves—a narrative that takes you from where you came and shows you to where you might go.

These are the fundamental elements of a story you can share with a potential employer, your spouse, a close friend, or anyone else who might ask, "What are you doing now and where are you going? Why are you doing this?"

Review each of these documents thoroughly. Consider what they are telling you about yourself, your past, your current situation, and your future. Once you are familiar and comfortable with your story, it is time to move on to the next chapter, "Cashing a Reality Check," where you will ask those who know you the best to give you some honest feedback on what you think you have learned about yourself.

CHAPTER 7

Cashing a Reality Check

Where is there dignity unless there is honesty?

—Cicero

At this stage of the process, you have completed the key self-assessment portions of A.I.M. You will have reviewed them and begun to develop an understanding of your "story," a narrative based on reflection and self-examination. In doing so, you have identified your central challenge, looked at your motivations, values, and past experiences, and then brainstormed about some options you might like to explore.

At this point, the next logical step would seem to be that you should immediately begin exploring the new directions that you have identified. You have moved from perhaps feeling frustrated and stuck in the mud to glimpsing a new world of understanding and possibility. Why not move ahead and begin to act on it right away? Have you determined that you might want to start your own business? Well, there's no time like the present—let's start setting it up! Have you identified that you are stuck in an unhappy job or relationship that is just an extension of past failures? If we've identified a new direction that breaks that pattern, let's get to it!

These are all logical steps that one might think are appropriate at this stage. **And they are completely wrong.** If you were to immediately act on your analysis to date, you would run the significant risk that you will go off in a direction that may be completely unsuited to you.

People are fallible. We often make mistakes, and in many cases, our mistakes are the product of closed thinking—thought processes that we keep completely to ourselves. In these closed loops, we can rationalize anything. We often use reference points and knowledge about ourselves that is completely internal. In doing so, we often ignore things that are obvious to others, because we are entirely unconscious of them. The fish, as the saying goes, sees everything but the water. For our part, we often see things that are far in the distance or obsess about small things, while completely ignoring a major issue that is right in front of us, staring us in the face.

Why? Because most people are often completely oblivious to their own weaknesses and predispositions. A small measure of this can often be a good thing. If we constantly thought about our own limitations, we might undermine our confidence or might never strike out in a new direction. If we were to make major life decisions, however, without the benefit of an outside perspective, we might end up making a decision that is completely unsuitable for us.

My co-author, Alex, for example, loves surfing. When he talks about the feeling of complete relaxation that comes from trying to work with the wind and the waves, he gets very animated. It is clear that surfing is something that he would like to do more often if he lived on one of the coasts. I also know that if anyone suggested he should start a professional surfing career, he would quickly laugh and say something like, "I would definitely like to surf more often, but there is no way I would ever be good enough to be a professional. That's just not a realistic choice for me."

But imagine if Alex didn't have a realistic perception of his own abilities in this area? Imagine if he were doing A.I.M. for the first time and discovered that he liked surfing more than many of the other things he did. What if he had identified "professional surfer" as a possible option in his future list and became incredibly excited about it? If he were to go directly from that realization to immediately explore this option, he might expend considerable time and resources trying to chase a dream that, in the end, just wasn't that realistic for him.

That is why A.I.M. builds in a very important step at this stage of the process. We call it "cashing a reality check." We have spent the stages prior to this one focusing inwards, asking ourselves questions we might not normally ask about what we want, what we value, and where we want to go in the future. Now it is time to let others in on the process, asking them to give us feedback on our thinking thus far. In doing so, you will look for a "reality banker" with whom you can cash your reality check. This should be a person who knows you very well, someone who can give you a frank and realistic assessment of what you are thinking, suggest alternate ideas, and offer comments about your discoveries. This will either give you a confidence boost that you are on the right track, or give you valuable insight that can help you refine your assumptions and reflections.

Choosing the right "reality banker"

Through my coaching experience, I have seen clients choose their trusted advisors from a very interesting list. Some have thought long and hard about it and approached several candidates before finding the right person; others have quickly named an advisor who was a perfect fit. In every case, however, their advisors have added value to their journey through the A.I.M. process, helping them make better and more informed decisions about their choices and their futures.

On one occasion, a client took all of three seconds to pick an advisor—and it was an excellent choice. Hans was a forty-five-year-old executive for a pharmaceutical company who was facing some serious challenges at a key point in his career. We had been progressing quite well through the initial stages of the A.I.M. process for several weeks, and it was now time for him to cash his reality check.

We met in my office but, unusually, he had brought his wife along. They were attending a theater performance after our meeting and, as they had a very open and trusting relationship, he had invited her to sit in on our meeting and hear what he and his coach had been working on.

After reviewing his progress to date, I explained that he now needed to pick a reality banker, someone who knew him well and could provide objective feedback on his thoughts about the challenges he faced. Hans paused for a few seconds, turned to his wife and said, "You know me better than anyone else. What do you think?"

If she was surprised by his choice, she didn't show it. After a minute or so, she voiced, very accurately, what she thought her husband needed to do.

"You've achieved a great deal in your career so far, but you haven't received the benefits from all of that hard work. You've allowed yourself to be taken advantage of by others. You now need to stand up for yourself. When I look at your career options, you are an expert in financial analysis and you have a good track record in your industry. Of the options you have sketched out, I can see you either consulting or taking on another senior position at another company. In either case, I know you value financial stability, so any of the riskier options you have looked at will cause you a lot of stress if you choose to take them. Speaking personally, I'd like us to spend more time together and—most importantly—I want you to feel good about yourself instead of feeling defeated by your job."

With that, she sat back in her chair and folded her hands in her lap. Mission accomplished.

I was stunned, but pleased. I had seen elements of her analysis in our work to date, but she had accurately taken her knowledge of Hans and tied everything together in a few sentences. It was obvious that she had been waiting months, if not years, to say this to him. The great part about this breakthrough was that he quickly agreed with all of her advice!

"Joan, you're absolutely right," he said. "I do need to be a little more selfish when it comes to my career. And I do value financial security, so the riskier options I was considering might not be the best fit for me. Jim, let's do some more work on the other options we considered."

They left my office for the theater with a bounce in their steps. I was a little stunned, but pleased that he had made such progress. Other clients have taken weeks or months to reach the point that Hans had reached in just 5 minutes.

This is not to say that your partner should be your first choice. In my experience, it is quite rare for my coaching clients to opt to make their spouse their reality banker. In most cases, they want to keep their personal and professional challenges separate from their family life. It also goes without saying that it is completely unrealistic for anyone else to expect to progress through the reality check phase in 5 minutes. Yet Hans's story is illustrative of the type of feedback you should try to solicit from whomever you choose as your reality banker—honest, direct, and informed by a deep knowledge of who you are and what might make you happy.

Many of my other clients have chosen their past professional mentors—people they have turned to in previous years to help guide them in their careers. Mentors generally have considerable life experience and can be objective, because they don't have a professional or personal stake in your career. In their role as reality banker, they are called upon to advise rather than to judge, and, consequently, they often offer an excellent, and sometimes unexpected, perspective on your challenges.

This was perhaps most evident with Daniel, another of my clients who worked as a chief operating officer for an auto parts firm. Daniel had asked William, his longtime mentor, to serve as his reality banker. Daniel was nearing fifty-five, and was facing two major issues. While he was satisfied with his current position, he was having a challenge making his work more enjoyable. He was also facing retirement in the next ten years and wanted to begin preparing himself for that transition.

In the early stages of the A.I.M. process, Daniel realized that his challenges did not require immediate action and that he could address them over a number of years. His sense of purpose was clear and, as we moved forward together, he regularly consulted his mentor about various options that we had uncovered.

William, his mentor, was the retired CEO of a Fortune 100 company. A kind man, he had known Daniel for more than twenty years and had always been a solid and reliable source of advice and counsel. With his own retirement still fresh in his memory, William could also relate to the questions Daniel was now asking himself.

In their first meeting, he reaffirmed that Daniel was on the right track in considering his retirement options at the age of fifty-five. While William was comfortable with his own decision to retire well after the age of sixty-five, he commended Daniel for taking such a proactive approach to his future. He was also able to provide some valuable perspective on some areas that Daniel had not yet considered as possible options after retirement. William knew that Daniel and his wife had a personal connection to a local cancer charity, so he suggested that Daniel explore becoming involved in the board of a nonprofit organization. He also suggested that Daniel investigate other interests that he had mentioned over the years, suggesting Daniel may want to consider teaching at a local community college. After his own retirement, William had continued to do consulting work for companies in his former area of expertise, and asked Daniel to explore how he might adapt that approach to his own post-retirement strategy.

As Daniel's case shows, mentors can make a coach's job considerably easier. In effect, Daniel benefitted from having a second coach, someone who could supplement the process he was going through in an empathetic manner, informed by his or her own encounter with similar life experiences.

In addition to spouses or mentors, other clients have chosen a range of reality bankers, including friends, peers, and current/past bosses. If you choose this route and go beyond those people whom know you intimately, you have to ask yourself whether they know you well enough to provide genuine perspective. Are they willing to deliver "bad news" if you need to hear it? True friends are those who will tell you things that you might not want to hear; so, the last person you need to help you cash a reality check is someone who will be reluctant to upset you by telling you that you may be heading in a questionable direction. With peers or work colleagues, there are other factors to consider. They may be facing challenges similar to your own and, therefore, may not have enough distance from the issue to provide objective advice. Because they are operating in the same environment, they may not be able to offer a perspective that is much different than your own. With a former boss, you may want to question whether that person would be able to relate to you independent of the formal relationship you have both had. In both of these cases, you may want to ask yourself whether such people will be able to provide you with the honest perspective that this stage of A.I.M. demands.

Getting the right reality banker: Sandra and Patrick's stories

Sandra was a forty-two-year-old, mid-level banking executive who was recommended to me by a former colleague. When I met Sandra, she was at a stage in her career where she felt that she wasn't moving forward quickly enough, and was spending too much time "fighting fires" for her superiors and not enough time on the quality projects that would help her build a solid corporate reputation.

She had come to me after a less-than-successful attempt to address her issues with a mentor. In the past, Sandra had come to rely on this person for support, so she had gone to him with her concerns, asking for his advice about what to do to move her career and life forward. Unfortunately, in the course of a brief meeting, he immediately recommended a number of short-term solutions that she should undertake right away. Sandra immediately attempted to put these ideas into action, but they quickly stalled, leaving her frustrated, confused, and more than a little desperate.

"Jim," she explained in our first meeting, "I've already tried and failed. I'm just really not that sure I can do this."

It took a few meetings for Sandra to overcome her doubts that she could really change her circumstances. But after taking the time to complete the first few A.I.M. exercises, Sandra was able to identify a number of options and pursue them in a logical, focused manner, leading her to a new job where she began to quickly move up the ladder.

Your relationship to your possible mentor may also offer some complications. One of my former clients, Patrick, had asked his boss to be his reality banker. Patrick was a young engineering executive who had moved from a large company to a smaller, more entrepreneurial one. He began working with me to help him plot how this position fit within his broader life and career plans. He chose the owner of his new firm, a longtime colleague, to fill the advisor role.

For the most part, Patrick progressed well through the A.I.M. process with the exception of his relationship with his mentor. The continually shifting demands of a smaller, entrepreneurial company often got in the way of their relationship and of his mentor providing the truly independent advice that Patrick needed. I helped him manage the transition to another advisor, a consulting colleague of mine who really understood the challenges of adapting to an entrepreneurial company. With this new perspective, Patrick could now move ahead with his development, while not clouding his reporting relationships within his company with other elements that were not related to his position.

In these examples, we have seen how important it is at this stage of the A.I.M. process to have someone outside your world provide an independent and realistic assessment of your thinking up to this point. Now, let's look at how you can find, brief, and begin working with your own advisor to cash your own reality check.

Finding your own reality banker

It is now time for you to find your own reality banker—an advisor you can trust to look at the work you have done so far in the A.I.M. process, and give you an independent, honest perspective about it. Many coaching clients often find this stage challenging. While people have dozens of different friends and colleagues, it is often difficult to identify one or two that meet the following criteria:

- **Objective:** The person should be open-minded and a possibility-oriented thinker. Avoid anyone who thinks negatively or who might immediately say such things as: "Why would you want to do *that*?" or "I would never want to go there!"

- **A good listener:** We all have friends who talk more than they listen and often use conversations as a one-way flow of information, allowing you to only talk briefly before regaling you with story after story about themselves. It goes without saying that this type of person rarely makes a good reality banker. Instead, look for someone who will listen carefully and give you the chance to speak your mind.

- **Has known you for a long time:** Friends and colleagues come and go. If you were to look back at past stages of your life and career, you would probably find that many of the people you knew at any one time have fallen by the wayside. Someone you know and trust today may not have known you five years ago, or may not know you five years from now. In your reality banker, look for someone who has known you across different stages of your life and can, therefore, offer perspective informed by a number of years of personal knowledge.

- **Mature:** Has the person that you are considering had many life experiences of their own? If you are considering a significant change in your life, it would be valuable to have, as your advisor, someone who has been through several similar changes of their own.

- **Knows you personally *and* professionally:** An ideal advisor should know different aspects of your personality and be able to provide feedback about how potential directions and ideas will impact the "whole you." While such a person would be ideal, if you do not know someone who knows you in this way, you may need to find two separate individuals.

- **Honest:** In beginning the A.I.M. process, you have made a commitment to explore your options. If you have been brave enough to ask questions of yourself, to consider what could be very different options for your life, and to share those ideas with someone else, you need that person to be equally committed to providing you with honest and objective feedback.

- **Constructive:** It will also not be enough for your advisor to question your ideas, that individual should be able to challenge your thinking and offer different perspectives that you may not have considered.

Does this person sound superhuman? Not really. When my coaching clients consider these criteria and then think about all of the people they know, they are often surprised at how many of their colleagues and friends fit the bill.

How do you begin the search process? Start with your address book—either physically or on-line—and identify a "first cut" or a list of people who meet some of the criteria. Think back to past jobs you may have held, neighborhoods you may have lived in, houses of worship you may have attended, places you may have volunteered, etc. Feel free to ask your partner or close friends who they think you know well enough who might be able to fill the advisor role. As we will examine in Chapter Nine, every person is at the center of a number of distinct "networks" that they can call upon to help them. Be generous in your first list—include a wide range of people and then winnow them down to a few distinct candidates.

Once you have identified a list of those people you think meet at least some of the criteria, review the list with the following three key questions in mind:

1. Does this person **know me well enough** to assess where I am right now, what I am facing, and the options I have developed with respect to moving in a new direction?
2. Does this person have a **depth of experience and knowledge**, different than my own, which will allow him/her to give me some good advice and offer me suggestions that I may not have thought of?
3. Will this person be **honest and direct** enough to tell me if I am considering a direction that is absolutely not suited to me?

Your goal in reviewing the list is to identify two to three people who you feel are the "best of the bunch." Once you are comfortable with your final list, you now have to ask them to serve as your advisor.

In this task, we will use a lesson we will put to good use later in the A.I.M. process when we discuss networking. One of the prime issues in networking is that for each person you contact, there must be a sense of purpose. It must be readily apparent to the person you are contacting *why* you are contacting them and what it is that you want them to do. In this sense, this exercise is a great "dress rehearsal" for some of the calls and e-mails you will make in the networking phase of A.I.M.

Before you call or e-mail, rehearse on paper or on your computer screen exactly what you want to say. The following, for example, is a sample "opener" you may want to adapt for your own call or e-mail:

> "Hi, Susan. I would like to grab 30 minutes of your time to get your advice and input on some options I am considering with respect to my career/life/etc. Although I am pretty happy doing what I am doing right now, for many reasons, which I will explain when we get together, this is a good time for me to explore my options. You have known me for some time and I trust your opinion, so I think you would be a great sounding board for me."

You will notice that this statement, in just a few sentences, clearly states your purpose in contacting them, why you have contacted them, why it is important, and what you want them to do.

At this stage of the process—and in the networking stage—many of my coaching clients feel that asking others for help is an imposition. "I feel awkward asking them to help me," they say. "Suppose they say no?" First, once you have narrowed down your potential advisor pool to two or three good candidates, the chances that they will say "no" are very low. If someone meets most or all of the criteria we have outlined, chances are that they value your friendship and would be more than willing to help you with any challenge you face. Second, in the unlikely event that they decline or say they might feel uncomfortable playing this role for you, don't be discouraged. Receiving a "no" is not a reflection on you—it is, more often than not, a reflection of the busy schedule of your potential advisor, their comfort level with talking about personal issues, or other related matters. In the unlikely event that they do decline, simply thank them for considering it and move on to the next candidate.

Once your prospective advisor has agreed to serve in that role and you have set up a time for your first meeting, you might want to follow up by sending him an e-mail with a copy of the exercises that you have completed so far, along with a note to explain what they are. This should save some time in your initial meeting and give your advisor some background on the process, your thoughts, and the purpose of the meeting. It is important for you to come to your first meeting with your advisor with an open mind—ready to hear and accept any feedback he or she might have to offer.

A final story of a valuable reality check: Henry's correction

In our previous chapter, you will remember the story of Henry and how he had identified four different options that he wished to pursue. Based on his earlier exercises—windowpane, decade review, strengths and weaknesses list, and future options list—each of the options made perfect sense and were all feasible areas to explore further. Henry had next turned his attention to finding an advisor and, after following the process outlined above, identified several people who could play that role.

He first opted to talk with just one person. Matt was a former colleague who he considered a close friend. In addition to working together for several years prior to Matt's move to a competing firm, they still played hockey together once a week. After discussing this choice with me, Henry asked Matt to serve as his advisor. Matt, appreciating the importance of Henry's request and knowing a little about his current circumstances, quickly agreed.

At their first meeting, Henry later told me that Matt had been forthright from the start. "I reviewed the materials you sent me in advance," Matt said. "But I want to hear it from you—what are you doing and how can I help you with it?"

Henry responded by leading Matt through the exercises he had completed, logically hitting the highpoints of the "story" he had begun to put together using them. He closed with the four options he had identified and asked Matt, point blank, to give him his honest feedback on each of them.

"Matt," he said, "based on these exercises, I've identified four possible options that I want to explore. You've known me for some time and we work in the same field. What do you think of these options as a fit for me?"

Matt nodded, but added one additional question. "Henry," he replied, "I think this is a great idea and I am more than willing to help you here. But before we review these, I need to know what your wife and family think about all this? Are you going down this path alone, or are they supporting you to make this change?"

Henry was a little taken aback by the question, but quickly realized where Matt was coming from. Their two families were quite close, seeing each other a few times a year and even vacationing together on occasion. More than any other advisor, Matt could appreciate how much Henry valued his family. His question, while unexpected, was welcomed. Henry referred back to the windowpane exercise, explaining that he had completed it with his wife's help and had explained to her that the A.I.M. process might result in major changes to their lives.

"Helen is behind me in this," Henry explained. "She trusts me to make the right choice for me and her and the kids."

With that, Matt and Henry were on the same page. They spent the better part of the next hour reviewing each of the possible options that Henry had presented. With respect to staying with his current company, they discussed the risks of championing a possible merger and what this might mean to his position with his colleagues. Matt offered some valuable advice on other people in Henry's current company whom he might talk with about the possibility of the firm being sold. He also confirmed that there was open talk in the industry about when—not if—the firm would be acquired, validating what Henry was seeing from the inside.

When they discussed Henry's possible move to a similar company, Matt talked about his own experience in moving from Henry's firm. He confirmed that he had faced challenges in building a reputation within a new firm where he was relatively unknown, but offered some advice on how Henry might overcome that. He also offered some suggestions about other people that Henry might talk to about opportunities with other firms.

Matt's value to Henry as an advisor was most evident, however, when they discussed his final options—joining a consulting practice or pursuing more entrepreneurial ventures. In his current position, Matt frequently hired consultants to work on various projects, so he was familiar with their skills and methods. Based on this perspective, Matt agreed that Henry's years of experience and his specific skill set would make him very valuable as a consultant. This was confirmed as they both reviewed Henry's strengths and weaknesses list in the context of the skills that would make for a successful consultant. Matt highlighted Henry's commitment to professionalism, his desire to work in teams, and ability to multitask. He noted, however, that while Henry had considerable experience, he had only worked with one firm, so he may find that many of the ways in which his current firm worked would be different than those of potential consulting clients. He also raised the extensive travel that was often part of consulting life and the impact that might have on Henry's family. Matt then offered to connect Henry with a few of the consultants he regularly engaged, so that Henry could learn more about the consulting lifestyle and whether it might be a good fit.

When they discussed moving to a more entrepreneurial situation, Matt threw Henry a definite curveball by asking him a simple question. "Henry, tell me who you work for right now."

Henry was puzzled, but quickly responded, "You know who I work for. I work for XYZ Company as the director of . . ."

Matt held up a hand to interrupt him, smiling. "Henry," he said, "that will be a major problem for you if you want to go out and explore working on your own. Entrepreneurs don't work for anybody—they work for themselves. Are you ready to think like that? Or will you be more comfortable working for someone else?"

Henry was stunned by Matt's question. His first reaction was that his good friend was telling him he shouldn't consider becoming an entrepreneur. In their subsequent discussion, however, Matt clarified that he was merely pointing out that Henry might not know enough about the mindset of an entrepreneur and he may want to explore that further if he wanted to consider whether it was a viable option, weighing the risks and rewards along with whether he had the personal orientation necessary for a more entrepreneurial environment.

Henry's experience with Matt shows the value a good advisor can add to the A.I.M. process at this stage. Had he not met with Matt, he might have charged off into a new job with a smaller firm without considering all of the ramifications. He may also have dismissed his concerns about the possibility his firm might be sold, saying, "That's just me thinking. I'm sure that won't happen." Matt confirmed that his company was, in all likelihood, a takeover target, validating the very purpose of Henry beginning the A.I.M. process in the first place.

Moving forward from your reality check

Like Henry, cashing a reality check should provide you with some new perspective on your process and the options you have identified. Are you satisfied that your reality banker has not "pussyfooted" around? Are you satisfied that you've been given some direct feedback—perhaps something you did not expect? Has he or she suggested new directions you might not have considered or offered other contacts that can help you further explore your options?

If so, add their feedback to your documents, noting any questions that remain outstanding or new areas you need to explore or clarify. As you move forward, be sure to keep your reality banker advised of your progress.

You are now ready to progress on to assess the options you have identified, determining which ones are most viable, and then move into the final stages of A.I.M.

CHAPTER 8

Asking the Hard Questions

It is better to know some of the questions than all of the answers.

—James Thurber

Just as human beings are often oblivious to their own strengths and weaknesses and the opportunities they may be ignoring, they are also often unable to ask themselves the hard questions at the important times in their lives. Everyone, for example, has friends who have suffered through failed relationships or made bad career choices. On reflection, they often say, "Well, it's partially my fault. I knew this issue might be a problem early on. I was just too caught up in everything else to want to deal with it then." Others may have had doubts or been cautioned about a particular career choice, a move to another city, or the start of a new sport or pastime. But in such cases, they—like most of us—probably brushed aside these nagging doubts in a rush to *do* something, in the rush to *act* and *move* and *explore*.

Instead, at times when people are considering major changes in their lives, the most important thing they can do is ask rational and measured questions about the actual *viability* and *practicality* of the choices they are considering.

Earlier in the A.I.M. process, for example, you may have identified that your spouse and family are very important to you. As the main breadwinner, you are cognizant of your responsibility to meet their needs. It may also be the case that one of your favored options may require that you return to school, take several years out of the workforce, and move to another city. Even if you are incredibly passionate about life change, it would be foolish to begin devoting time and energy towards exploring this option without first asking some rational questions about the impact it would have on your personal life and your ability to support your family.

You may also have identified many different and diverse options, any of which would require a large commitment of your time. If you immediately began to explore all of them, you would quickly realize that you do not have enough spare time to give each of them fair consideration. By not asking questions to narrow down the field or determine which ones would be more important or the most practical, you might spend two or three months researching a variety of options and learning very little. This, in turn, could leave you disillusioned and angry at having wasted so much time with no tangible results, a marked contrast to the quick progress you may have made in the earlier stages of A.I.M. if you had spent some time to identify your various paths forward.

You get the picture. That is why, at this stage of the A.I.M. process, you will ask yourself several pointed questions about the options you have identified. Through these questions—and your answers to them— you'll be able to allocate a certain percentage of the time you have available to explore your options. The goal is to ensure that you do not try to do too much and end up by doing very little. This process will also ensure that you spend the limited amount of time that you have on the options that have the greatest chance of success and which, practically, have the most impact on the challenges you have identified.

The FIVE key questions you need to ask NOW to save grief LATER

At this stage of the A.I.M. process, my clients are usually feeling confident. They have learned a great deal about themselves and have taken the time to consider, in a rigorous manner, how past experiences relate to their current challenge. They have also identi-fied a number of potential options and gone through the important step of identifying a reality banker and asking him or her to provide feedback on their choices. By cashing a reality check you may already have started to ask yourself some of the questions we will deal with in the following pages.

As we have done in other stages, begin this stage with any mate-rials you have produced spread out on a table in front of you. Closest to you, place your future options list—that's the paper, divided into columns, that outlines areas you would like to explore as you move forward. Beneath the columns you already have outlined, add five new rows and title them "passion," "good at it," "windowpane fit," "cost," and "time."

As an example, here is the list that Henry completed with the additional (blank) new rows added:

HENRY'S FUTURE OPTIONS LIST	Staying where I am?	Another big company?	Smaller, entrepreneurial company?	Join a consulting practice?
	Stick it out and take my chances, since I have been treated well, there is no reason to think my successful career path should not continue.	The head-hunters tell me I am in demand, so maybe there is another big company out there that might give me more freedom.	I am intrigued about this possibility, as I have seen friends who have made this kind of move, and they seem to feel fulfilled and their ideas are being appreciated.	With my experience in operations and planning, is this the time to go into consulting and enhance my skills even more, probably with a large consulting shop that houses "best practices in my field?"
Ideal role	Current position	Similar position to current	Unknown	Unknown
Passion				
Good at it				
Windowpane fit				
Cost				
Time				

With these additions to your future options list in front of you, now think about the following five questions:

1. Which option(s) am I most passionate about?

One of the logical statements that underlies the A.I.M. process is a simple one: There are a great many things we can spend our limited amount of time doing, so we should choose to do those things that we enjoy and feel passionate about instead of those that may bore or discourage us.

When you performed the brainstorming exercise in Chapter Five to develop your future options list, you were tasked with getting it all on paper and not worrying about the "buts or barriers." We did not ask you to rank the options or indicate if you favored some over others. Now that you have all of your options before you and have begun to do some background work on each of them, it is time to evaluate each option to determine which ones you feel most strongly about. On the surface, which ones excite you or are you passionate about? If you had to tell a friend or family member, "I am thinking about doing X!"—with "X" being the option that makes you the most excited.

One of my former clients offered an excellent example of how exploring his passion produced unexpected results. I became Ed's coach several years ago, when, at a high point in his career, he had developed doubts about whether he was actually doing what made him most happy. Ed had trained as an engineer, but as he moved into the corporate world, his outgoing personality coupled with his technical knowledge saw him move into sales. When we met, he was a forty-seven-year-old senior sales manager for a financial services company and he had recently completed his MBA. Ed's company regarded him highly—he had received several recent promotions—and he seemed poised to move into a VP position in the coming years.

There was only one problem—and it was a big one. When I asked Ed to tell me about himself, one of the first things he said was, "I'm good at what I do, but I don't think it makes me happy any more."

The work he did moving through the first few stages of the A.I.M. process reinforced his initial doubts. It became clear that Ed was passionate about engineering, about building things, and getting into the nuts and bolts of what made things work. He became incredibly excited when he shared that, as a child, he had watched construction sites for hours just to follow the work, each day marveling at how a building was put together, layer by layer. When it came time to identify his future options list, one of the areas was clear: Could he find a smaller, entrepreneurial, engineering-related company that would make use of both his passion for the profession as well as his business and sales experience?

Putting the later stages of A.I.M. into practice, Ed used his network to connect with the owner of a small construction materials firm who, coincidentally, was looking for someone to take over his business. Armed with an introduction from a friend, Ed met the owner and, after delivering a good elevator speech (which you will develop in Chapter Ten), they began serious talks. The owner was impressed with Ed's combination of sales experience and his passion about engineering, and the two soon came to a deal. Ed is now learning the ropes of this new business and is happier than I have ever seen him.

"Jim," he said when we last met, "I can't believe what a difference it makes to work in an area that you're really passionate about."

2. Which option(s), realistically, am I most likely to be good at?

In our rush to explore our dreams, we often forget about one crucial thing—it is hard to be happy doing something that you will never be good at.

In the previous chapter, I offered the example of my co-author Alex's passion for surfing. He is truly enthusiastic about it, and if he were considering a life change and had identified becoming a professional surfer as a possible future option, he would probably be able to find some spare time to explore it further. It might be a good fit with his original windowpane exercise. He may even be able to justify the costs of taking time away from his growing consulting practice. But if he were to ask the simple question of whether he is likely to become sufficiently good enough at surfing to make his living as a surfer, he would quickly admit that the answer would be "no."

One of my former clients underwent a similar realization when she chose to explore a career in the medical field.

When I met Patricia, she was a banking executive in her mid-forties who was considering a career change. Her main concern was this: While she was good at her job and well liked by her staff and colleagues, she felt her job did little to engage the compassionate side of her personality.

"Jim," she said in our first meeting, "I'm a caring person and I want to help other people. Looking at numbers all day just doesn't give me the room to do that."

As we moved through the various A.I.M. exercises, I learned that Patricia greatly admired her father, a family doctor who had been loved by his patients and respected in the community in which she grew up. In addition to her father, Patricia had several other close relatives who were doctors. They had always been passionate about their profession, and she wondered whether she had missed an opportunity to follow in their footsteps, choosing a path that would allow her to help people while, at the same time, make a decent living and supporting her family.

When we began talking about her options, she immediately said she wanted to look at leaving the executive ranks at the bank, enter medical school, and become a doctor. We discussed the pros and cons of such a radical move as much as we could, raising a number of questions. How long might it take to get a medical degree? How likely was it that Patricia might fail in such a transition? Would she be able to juggle the demands of her family obligations with the long hours of studying and eventual residency? And was she suited to the types of work that doctors do every day?

Through networking, Patricia connected with a few doctors with whom she could discuss, very practically, the pros and cons of her possible career shift. After two long discussions where she gathered considerable information about their daily workload and the amount of time it would take her to qualify to become a doctor, Patricia realized that her idea was not feasible. She did, however, identify a number of other roles in the healthcare sector that could help her put her compassion into action, which were more compatible with her family obligations and could build on her executive experience at the bank. Patricia went on to explore leadership positions in various health charities and agencies—options she might not have considered had she not explored, and ruled out, her first choice of becoming a doctor.

3. Which of these options fit best with my windowpane?

In Chapter Four, we mapped the four-dimensional you with respect to the personal, professional, spiritual, and physical aspects of your life. In each of these areas, you were asked to be honest about how you saw yourself and noted what you valued in each of these four quadrants. You may even have included additional information in the panes during the subsequent stages of the process, as your work to sketch success and discuss your findings with your reality banker may have brought other ideas to the fore.

Now it is time to review what you have identified in this four-quadrant exercise and compare those points to the options that are before you. Are there any that are obvious fits? Is there information that indicates that some choices would be preferable to others? Are there any flashing red lights that seem to say, "Don't consider this one!" when looking at all of them? If so, please note your comments in the appropriate row.

My work with Roger underlies the importance of ensuring that the choices you explore should mesh well with what you have learned about your values through the windowpane exercise. I first met Roger, a partner in a professional services firm, when he was in his early fifties. I had been called in because he and his partners were at an impasse. While he was technically brilliant at what he did, he was widely viewed as a difficult guy to work with.

"Jim, they think I'm a curmudgeon." Roger said to me in our first meeting, without any hint of irony or humor. "They see me as a stick in the mud who won't go along with what they want to do, but I have principles that I have to stand behind. If they can't respect those, to hell with them."

I didn't need a crystal ball to figure out that this kind of inflexibility on Roger's part was not a good trait in a partnership environment. Professional services firms, whether they are dentists, lawyers, doctors, or consultants, are places where progress is only possible if those involved are committed to agreement, compromise, and open discussions. Roger's attitude would be a problem in such an environment.

Roger's future options list had identified a few areas he wanted to explore. He was interested in moving to another firm, provided they would welcome his principles-based approach. He was also interested in pursuing a more technical position with one of his firm's previous clients or striking out on his own to open his own consulting practice. Roger's initial research identified opportunities in each of these areas, which led to a very poignant conversation with me concerning which ones he would prioritize.

As we reviewed his options list together, he kept qualifying what another company would have to do to make him happy. Among many of the things he mentioned were statements such as the following:

- They'll have to realize I work out of my home office whenever I want.
- I don't have time for useless staff meetings; they'll have to respect that.
- I don't have time to negotiate salary; they'll just have to meet my demands.

This was a good opportunity for me to bring up his windowpane exercise, where he had emphatically said he was unwilling to compromise on his principles. "Roger," I said to him, "if having your own way is very important to you, why do you want to explore working for someone else? Isn't the logical thing to look at how you can work for yourself and build a successful business around that?"

He looked me straight in the eye and glowered a bit, but then dropped his gaze. "Jim, you're right," he said. "I've had a hard enough time getting my current partners to compromise. What chance would I have with an entirely new bunch?"

With this realization in hand, Roger concentrated on transitioning from his existing firm and setting up an independent consulting practice. He put his elevator speech together, went back to his partners, and talked about how they could build a different kind of relationship that would see him move out on his own. I ran into Roger a few years later and found that he was enjoying his independence, while working on a steady flow of projects.

"Jim, I'm still a curmudgeon," he said, laughing this time, "but now I don't have to apologize to anyone."

4. Which of these options can I afford to explore?

One of the things about living, as the saying goes, is that it costs money. Few of us are wealthy enough to be able to ignore financial pressures while we pursue self-fulfillment. Most of us have a mortgage to service, kids and a partner to please, weekly and monthly bills to pay, and retirement to save for. If one of the goals of the A.I.M. process is to transition to a new lifestyle in some form or other, we still have to pay our bills while we make the necessary changes happen.

At this stage of the A.I.M. process, you have to ask yourself some blunt questions about the options you have identified: Can I really afford to pursue them? Are there some options that are less financially risky than others? What degree of financial risk can I tolerate—and for how long—as I pursue my dreams? What could each of these options cost me in terms of dollars and cents—and can I afford it?

This does not mean that the financial question is an "on-off switch" that can stop your change process in its tracks. Rather, you have to be honest about what certain options may cost you and think of ways to mitigate those costs if you really want to proceed with them.

The coaching I do for people who are pursuing a mid-career MBA offers a number of examples of how financial concerns can focus someone's direction in one way and not another. The clients that I see from that program are typically individuals who are financing it themselves. The price tag for the degree is in the high five figures, and the program can take fifteen to eighteen months to complete. In that time, they will have to devote up to thirty hours per week to their course work, sacrificing leisure and family time to do so. Many of them have to borrow the money or finance the program from their savings, meaning that they are generally very committed people with a high expectation that their investment will yield large returns.

Andy was one of the students I coached in the MBA program, and financial concerns were the deciding factor in which path he chose to explore. Andy was working for a small company when we first met, running their training and development division. A well-spoken man in his mid-thirties with a wife and young family, he had decided that he wanted more from life and had enrolled in an MBA program. By all accounts, he had acquitted himself quite well. His graduation date was nearing, however, and he now faced the choice of whether to return to his previous position or strike out in a new direction. He had enjoyed an income in the high five figures and his wife was just starting up her own consulting business. Essentially, they were living on his income and now faced the prospect of paying back the loan he had taken out for his tuition fees.

One of the options we uncovered as we moved through Andy's future options list was that he might want to open his own training business or go into business with his wife. She had very strong skills in teaching and training as well, so they were probably a good fit should they both decide to combine forces. Andy was interested in exploring the idea, which we did by first having a discussion with his wife—his likely business partner.

The three of us sat down and reviewed Andy's choices. His wife was very open to the idea, but as we discussed the work Andy had done through the A.I.M. process to date, one point kept coming up that indicated this might not be the best choice for them at this time. In his windowpane exercise, Andy had noted the financial stress of the MBA program in his personal quadrant, stating that he wanted to get out of debt as soon as possible. The more he and his wife discussed it, the more they realized that their major financial needs had to come first and that starting a business right now was simply too much of a financial risk.

Both Andy and his wife were comfortable with this decision, but they decided not to abandon the idea of starting a joint business altogether. Instead, they made the decision to merely change the timetable. His wife went ahead and started her own business, with occasional advice and input from Andy. He returned to his old job, but kept exploring his options with an eye towards eventually joining his wife in the business. Two years later, with his loans paid off, Andy did join her in the business, which continues to flourish.

5. How much time do I *honestly* have to devote to these options right now?

Technology has solved many problems for us over the years. We once sent letters across the country and waited weeks for a reply; now we send e-mails and trade text messages with those around the world instantly.

There is, however, one problem that technology has not been able to solve for us. No matter how advanced our society becomes, there will always be twenty-four hours in a day and we will need a portion of that to rest and replenish ourselves. This limitation on our time means that if we want to put the A.I.M. process into effect, we are limited by the amount of time we have. Most of us cram a significant amount into the sixteen to eighteen waking hours we have in a day—time with family, eating, running errands, physical activity, and, if you are employed, work. Into this already crowded mix, we are proposing to fit the process of exploration and rediscovery that is A.I.M.

At this stage in the A.I.M. process, people are anxious to get going. The first caution I offer is that they have less time than they think—so spend it wisely! Make a realistic assessment of how much time you can allocate to exploring all your options in a week, and then allocate that portion of your time to each of the options.

The case of appropriate time allocation was never more relevant than with Tim, a client I began coaching several years ago. He was a VP with a mid-size manufacturing firm in his early forties who was facing a possible career transition. Tim was a go-getter from the first meeting and blazed through the initial stages of A.I.M. When we arrived at his future options list, he quickly identified five areas that he wanted to explore. However, he wanted to explore all five of them right away—and this was a problem. Tim was like a kid in a candy store; he was not accustomed to having someone ask him to slow down to take the time to ensure he made the right choice.

The five options Tim identified were as follows:

1. Talk with headhunters so they can help me find a similar job with another manufacturing company.
2. Talk to friends of mine who are teaching in community colleges so I can move to teach either part time or full time in my field.
3. Talk to entrepreneurs that I know through my family who can help me set up my own business.
4. Get into the private equity business, as others have told me I would be good at it.
5. Write a book. I know folks who could tell me what it takes.

As you can see, any one of these options would require considerable work on Tim's part. My concern, as his coach, was that he would spread his attention across all five of these options and not do any one of them justice. When I shared this concern with Tim, he refused to consider it. I think I'm on safe ground when I say that he was not the most diplomatic client I have ever had, as evidenced by our discussion concerning his options. When I tried to get him to realistically assess how much time he might have to explore them, his first reaction was to dismiss my concerns.

"I have plenty of time," he said, "and if I don't have time, I will make it happen. Let's get going—you're wasting my time."

Reluctantly, I agreed. I knew there would be no dissuading him from his course of action, so I decided to let him try to explore all of them at the same time. When we met two months later, it was a very different, and humbled, person who sat down in the chair opposite my desk.

Tim was discouraged and confused. He had tried to explore all of his options, but since he hadn't focused on only a small number, he had spread himself too thin. He had not maximized his networking calls, nor had he done proper research with respect to any of them.

"It burns me to say this, Jim," he said, "but you were right. This is a big job and I . . ."

I politely cut him off there. "No need to apologize," I said. "Let's get to work.

We then proceeded to discuss each option, one at a time. By referring back to the previous work he had done in the A.I.M. process, and through a realistic assessment of the time he had available, we managed to narrow down his options to the field he knew the best—the manufacturing sector. In the time allocation on his matrix, Tim applied 100 percent of his free time to exploring opportunities with other firms. He arranged proper meetings with headhunters, we polished up his elevator speech in advance of those meetings, and he made the rounds. The result came several weeks later, when he called to tell me that he had found another, more challenging, position at a related company.

Keeping your momentum going—some tricks and tips

The A.I.M. process thrives on little victories, those small, yet rewarding, "wins" that keep you motivated and help you build momentum to keep going. To achieve these small victories, consider the following tactics that will help you spend your time wisely:

- If one of your options is to explore working for another company, identify just one prospect instead of several, and ask yourself what you want to find out about that firm: What do you know about its financial data? Who serves on the board of directors? Who makes up the executive team? How well regarded are their products, etc.? Next, address one area at a time, building a dossier of research about your new prospective employer and keep track of the amount of time it takes you. This will allow you to better gauge your time as you take on other tasks.

- If one of your priorities is to begin looking for another job in your current field, consider contacting one search consultant who works in your field, rather than contacting dozens of different companies. Career ads on the Internet and in newspapers often ask those interested in a position to contact a search consulting company, so an Internet search of past postings for positions similar to those you wish to apply for should help you to determine which firm does the most recruiting work in your field.

- Is the solution you are looking for a tactical one (e.g., find another job, earn more money) or is it broader ranging (i.e., figure out what I want to do with my life)? Your initial work with A.I.M. should give you clues to the answers, as should your windowpane exercise. In either case, identify the three most important things you can do to get the process moving and that you can do within a month—then do them.

How Henry's questions led to answers

Remember Henry? He was the engineering executive who was grappling with his prospects at his current firm, and figuring out whether he should explore other, outside options. When we left Henry's story in Chapter Six, he had completed the first stages of the A.I.M. process and had identified and assessed his potential options.

Henry then met his reality banker for detailed discussions on his options. His advisor affirmed that he was on the right track and gave Henry some valuable additional input. When we left Henry earlier in this chapter, he was working through the "hard questions" phase of A.I.M. using the following table:

HENRY'S FUTURE OPTIONS LIST	Staying where I am?	Another big company?	Smaller, entrepreneurial company?	Join a consulting practice?
	Stick it out and take my chances, since I have been treated well, there is no reason to think my successful career path should not continue.	The headhunters tell me I am in demand, so maybe there is another big company out there that might give me more freedom.	I am intrigued about this possibility, as I have seen friends who have made this kind of move, and they seem to feel fulfilled and their ideas are being appreciated.	With my experience in operations and planning, is this the time to go into consulting and enhance my skills even more, probably with a large consulting shop that houses "best practices in my field."
Ideal role	Current position	Similar to current position	Unknown	Unknown
Passion	Some.	Some.	Definitely.	Some.
Good at it	Yes.	Yes, if the job is similar.	Think I can do it.	I think my experience is transferable.
Windowpane fit	Yes; status quo and safe.	Some red flags, as it might disrupt things.	Could be high risk financially and personal strain.	Travel may be at odds with my family values.
Cost	No immediate cost to me.	Don't know my market value yet—it may be lower than where I am now.	If I have to put my own money into the firm, we can't afford that right now.	Unknown, but varying income levels of some consultants could upset our financial plans.
Time	None, as I have already committed the time.	I could explore this one with a few meetings.	This would take a big time commitment to explore, as I don't know this world.	A few meetings with the bigger firms should tell me if I am interested in this one.

As we can see from Henry's matrix, the option about which he was most passionate—a smaller entrepreneurial company—raised many other issues for him. The status quo, which he had set out to change, now didn't look so bad after all. After examining his options, Henry felt his choice was clear. "Jim," he shared with me after our session, "I'm going to stay where I am, but work towards making a move when I can afford to do it."

Henry continued to complete the A.I.M. process and built his network into a much better asset that could help him explore the world beyond his current employer.

Completing your own questions

With your own blank paper or screen in front of you, complete each of the sections outlined above. At the end of the process, you should have some indication of which options will take precedence over others, which ones you will devote the most time to, and, perhaps, which ones may require some additional clarification.

We are now ready to develop an in-depth road map for each option. This will involve, among other tasks, completing as much fact-finding as possible to help us narrow down the option(s) that really excite you and that you will, realistically, be able to achieve.

CHAPTER 9

Road Mapping Your Options

I have an existential map. It has "You are here" written all over it.

— Stephen Wright

Few people start out on a journey without figuring out the best way to get to their destination. You don't start a long road trip by jumping in the car and driving off minutes after you think a vacation might be a good idea. Generally, there is some planning involved. You will usually decide on a destination and have a discussion with your travel companions. Then you will probably pull out a few maps to determine where you might stop on your journey, and outline the best way to get you to your destination. If your traveling companions will include children, you might have to prepare yourself for a few questions like "Are we there yet?" coming from the back seat along the way. And, at some point, you are likely to trace your journey on a map with a marker, print off a final map from an on-line mapping system, or program your journey into a GPS. The map is a key part of a successful journey to your final destination.

So far, our work with the A.I.M. method has helped you to identify possible destinations that are a natural extension of your past and a good fit with your present. We have looked at what things you value and ensured your future options are compatible with them. In the preceding chapters, we have done considerable work to narrow down the possible options for your future and ensure they are compatible with both your abilities and values. The next step we will cover in this chapter is to take some time to create a "road map" of how you can best explore these options further.

Now that your future options have been reduced to a manageable number and you have decided which ones will take priority over others, it would seem that the natural next step would be to throw yourself wholeheartedly into investigating them. As we have seen in our various case studies, moving quickly to action is a natural human instinct. It is also an impulse that you have to restrain and moderate with a bit of additional work before you are ready to go out into the broader world and begin to explore your options.

In this chapter, you will learn how to apply two very misunderstood and underappreciated techniques—research and networking—to create a road map for exploring your options. By using these two techniques, you can map your most effective course forward, saving you both time and effort as well as increasing the chances that you will arrive at the destination you have identified.

Research: The starting point for all your options

Of all the things you can do to ensure success in any career or life transition, research is often the easiest step. Because research is easy, it is often overlooked, given short shrift, or not conducted properly at all.

Over the years, one of the main reasons I have seen my clients neglect or ignore basic research of their options is that they often assume they already know the answers to basic questions. As part and parcel of our bias to *act*—our rush to start doing something—we often assume we know things we really do not.

Let's say, as an example that your future options list has identified that you want to investigate moving to another company similar to your current employer. Your natural bias is to say, "If they are in

the same business as us, it must be roughly the same type of opera-
tion as the one I know." Yet General Motors and Toyota are in the
same business, right? Aren't Apple and Dell both computer manu-
facturers? Gap and Brooks Brothers are both clothing retailers,
aren't they? As you can appreciate, some basic research on the focus,
culture, and financial performance of these companies would tell
quite a different story.

Or suppose you have determined that you would like to move
to a new city as part of changing your life? You could assume that
cities of the same size should have the similar types of employers,
schools, and amenities. Well, Charlotte, NC, and Vancouver, BC,
are similar-sized cities, aren't they? Chicago, IL, is the same size as
Toronto, ON, isn't it? Internationally, London is the roughly same
size as New York. Well, you would only have to spend a day in any of
these cities to determine that they are quite different in many, many
ways, even though they are the same size.

You get the idea. Conducting basic research on your options is
a **must** before you begin exploring them. Done properly, research
will allow you to:

- Further refine your options, saving you time;
- Identify new areas to look within your options that you may
  not yet have considered;
- Give you background information so you know the right questions to ask when your networking begins; and
- Most importantly, good research will help you identify people who can help provide the answers you do not yet have for
  questions about your options, which is the key foundation
  for networking.

Moreover, conducting research is now easier than it was in previous years, thanks to technology. Through the wonders of Google,
a near-infinite list of potential data sources on any question is just a
few clicks away. The marvels of social media such as Facebook and
Twitter allow you to quickly engage a large number of people to ask
them questions about your research topic. On-line databases such as

LexisNexis, available through a university or local library, allow you to search media, financial reports, and thousands of different publications for information. All it requires is a bit of time—and knowing what questions to ask—to gather information that can greatly help your transition.

Naomi's research leads to a career transition

One of the best examples of using research to put a career and life change on solid ground came from a former client, Naomi. A tall, striking woman in her late forties, Naomi had come to me with very specific ideas about what she wanted to do with her career. She was a rising star in the corporate world—having already been a president three times in her career—and she was particularly adept at turning around troubled companies. This kind of challenge requires a very special type of executive, as it frequently entails some form of reorganization that challenges traditional structures and results, more often than not, with layoffs and aggressive cost cutting. Turning a company around is mentally and emotionally exhausting, requiring high energy, focus, and discipline. You cannot afford to be swayed emotionally, but instead remain focused on the tough job you were hired to do. To compound matters, your timeline for changing a company's direction is typically weeks or months—not years.

As successful as Naomi had been in these three situations, she was physically and emotionally exhausted when we met, and wanted to change the direction of her career. We spent many hours together during the first stages of the A.I.M. process, and by the time we arrived at the windowpane exercise, Naomi was able to quickly make some very specific points when reviewing the four dimensions of her current situation:

- I want to work with a domestic company. I feel patriotic and want to promote the advancement of companies from my own country. (Naomi had worked with three foreign-owned companies and was tired of reporting to people in other parts of the world.)

- I particularly enjoyed the time I spent interacting with people in the transportation business over the past several years, and would welcome an opportunity in that industry—especially if the company had an environmental angle, such as transit or commuter services.
- Although I would consider another role as president, it is not a must. I am worn out, so would welcome the opportunity to be part of a team and not be responsible for leading the charge.
- I would be happy to perform in an advisory capacity, such as a role in strategic planning or consulting.
- I am tired of traveling and would prefer to stay and work in the city in which I live now.

This was quite a definite, and very specific, list to have completed so early in the A.I.M. process. We were then able to do more work on her options, discussing them in our sessions and checking them out with her external reality banker and against the hard questions phase. In these discussions, we knew that Naomi had a definite desire to explore work in the transportation industry. Moreover, given her track record, there were only three possible roles she could seek in such a company: president, vice president of strategic planning or operations, or a senior external consultant to such a company. We also had a very specific location to explore, as Naomi did not want to move to another city, and she had also indicated a strong preference for a domestic, as opposed to a foreign, company.

These parameters were an excellent starting point for Naomi to begin her research process. She threw herself into researching her possible options. She was quickly able to identify transportation companies that were headquartered locally, and found several that were working in the field of commuter transportation. Narrowing her search even further, Naomi settled on three potential future employers: a company that manufactured buses; an Internet technology firm that made transportation software; and a third firm that was a transportation conglomerate.

As luck would have it, Naomi had already had some contact with the first two firms through her previous positions. She was able to supplement her knowledge with some additional research, and was then able to focus wholeheartedly on the firm with which she had no experience.

The company was publicly traded, so Naomi's starting point was to find and download its annual report. This, in turn, allowed her to learn more about their business, activities, key projects, strategic direction, the bios of the key executives, and a list of the board of directors. Most importantly, it allowed her to review the firm's audited financial statements, which showed her which business divisions were performing and which were struggling—facts she could easily determine by comparing the most recent statements with those from previous annual reports. Naomi was able to supplement this information with additional data gathered from press releases posted on-line, comments from bloggers and the investment community, and executive appointments that had been posted on-line and in the local business pages.

Taken together, Naomi's research gave her a very interesting picture of a potential future employer. She had learned that the company had several major business lines, including a commuter transportation company that their annual reports noted was the largest division in terms of sales and revenues. By comparing their financial statements year to year, however, she could see that the performance for this division had been declining over the past few years. The appointment notices and press releases told her that they had made some staff and operational changes in this division in response, but it did not seem to be having an impact on the results—a fact noted by a blogger who occasionally covered the company.

Naomi now had some detailed insight into this company that appeared to indicate it could use someone, in some capacity, with her turnaround talents. The picture the research had painted had piqued her interest, and she was curious to learn more about the challenges facing the company and whether she might have a role to play with respect to it.

With this preliminary research on the third company in hand, she could now compare it to the other two firms she had identified earlier. Her review of the first two firms showed little out of the ordinary; they were growing nicely, posting solid returns, and were well respected by others in the field, confirming what she knew from her contacts with both firms through her previous employer. Of her three prospects, her research now allowed her to focus on just one— the firm that appeared to have the greatest need for someone with her experience in turning around troubled firms. Moreover, this company was sufficiently large enough that she would not have to step into the president's job, with all its attendant stresses, in order to make a difference.

In order to take her research to the next level, it was now time for Naomi to talk with "real" people who actually knew what was going on with the company and whether there could be an opportunity for her. This would require mapping out a networking strategy—the next step in the road mapping phase of A.I.M.

Conducting your own research: Some tips

Like Naomi, you may want to consider the following starting points when conducting your own research:

- **The Internet** is everyone's best friend, whether you are choosing a restaurant for tomorrow night's dinner or researching a major change in your life. While popular search engines such as Google are good starting points, it is important to remember that certain websites will place higher than others when you perform keyword searches, depending on how well their programmers have "optimized" their search ability. As a backup, you may want to brainstorm for other organizations that are related to your search criteria and go directly to their websites. You can also look for portals on the general industry in which you are interested (Naomi, for example, could have looked at industry associations devoted to transportation) and follow the links on those sites to others. Additional online resources would include social networking sites (such as searching www.Facebook.com for groups dedicated to your topic) and popular blogging sites (such as www.Blogger.com or www.WordPress.com).

- **Libraries** have been in the research business since the time of the Greeks and Romans, and can be a valuable asset when collecting information. Of particular relevance are reference libraries (those that maintain larger collections of reference materials and databases) or those associated with universities or colleges (which generally have larger collections of materials). In any case, asking a librarian is always a good step—they have devoted their professional lives to cataloguing information and should be able to recommend places to look that you may not have considered.

Networking: The misunderstood technique

In all of my years in the coaching and employment search fields, I have found that networking is one of the most misunderstood concepts out there. Whenever the idea is raised in media articles and interviews about career management, so-called "experts" generally describe networking as simply "getting out there and meeting people." Armed with this idea, those who are new to networking generally begin calling other people and making appointments without putting much strategic thought into the *why* and *what* of the equation. Why have I picked this person to call? Why am I meeting with them? What is the purpose of the meeting? What do I want to say to them? What are my expectations of them, and them of me?

Without an in-depth understanding of what networking is and how it can really make a difference, too many people dismiss it as "just schmoozing, selling, and begging people for help." Others look down their nose at it, calling it "crass" or a tool for "salesmen and self-promoters," criticisms that both Alex and I have heard over the years.

From decades in this business, I can emphatically say they're wrong. In my experience as a professional coach, effective networking can be extremely useful as a lifelong way to manage a resilient career and life. It is particularly useful when you are planning a career shift or a major life transition.

Before we talk about why, it's important to understand exactly what effective networking looks like. In my opinion, networking can, and should, be a systematic way to obtain information from someone who can provide an answer, an interpretation, or a lead that will bring you to someone else who *does* have the answers. This can lead you to yet more answers and interpretations from more people. Eventually, you can combine all of the information and data you have gathered and develop an informed opinion or take a specific action.

When supporting the type of career or life transition that you have undertaken through the A.I.M. process, successful networking could be as simple as identifying two or three people through your research who would be best positioned to answer questions that are key to your transition. Through the techniques outlined in the following chapter ("Filling Up Your Toolkit"), you would schedule and hold meetings with these people, they would then answer your questions and introduce you to others who may also be able to help. If done properly, many of the people you contact could remain an ongoing part of a network that you can ask for advice and feedback throughout the remaining steps in your A.I.M. process and beyond.

The keys to successful networking are:

- Determine your expectations—the type of information you need from the meetings you are going to have.
- Identify whom you will approach for information.
- Develop the messages you want to deliver.
- Define the purpose of the requested meeting, the amount of time it will take, and your expectations.
- Set up and then conduct the meeting.
- Conclude the meeting by offering thanks for the individual's time and frankness.
- Send them a thank-you note for the meeting.
- Remain in touch as you move forward, if appropriate, giving them the chance to become part of your evolving network.

Naomi approached her networking strategy in as thorough a manner as she had done her background research. From her earlier work in the process, she had identified three possible companies to investigate further. The first two companies she already knew fairly well and could pick up the phone and talk with a number of people related to either of them. Her third prospect—the large firm that may have a problem with its transportation division—was another matter. Naomi did not know anyone connected to the firm, so she needed to develop a networking strategy from scratch to gather those personal details that would complement her background research.

As she considered whom she could speak with about the third company, Naomi came up with an interesting angle. As the company was publicly traded on the stock exchange, it was followed by various investment analysts who worked for different securities firms. Based on her previous experience leading public companies, Naomi knew several such analysts personally. So, the first step she identified in her networking strategy was to contact investment analysts and pick their brains about the company she had identified. The analysts could not talk directly about the company's culture or inside plans, but should be able to give her a perspective on its financial direction and overall health—particularly the declining revenues in the transportation division she had identified through her research. She also determined that she should ask each of the analysts for other contacts they knew outside the investment world who might be able to offer additional information and perspective on the company.

Naomi decided to talk to different consulting firms that might have been positioned to work for the company. Her purpose there was two-fold—she hoped to gain additional information on the company or additional contacts, and she was laying the groundwork for a possible consulting contract with one of the firms, should she identify that the best way she could help the company would be in an external role instead of joining its staff.

To round out her networking strategy, Naomi went ahead and met with the contacts she had identified in the first two companies. During the process of learning more about those two prospects, she was also able to gain some additional information on the third company. Her contacts were pleased to open other doors for more conversations in their respective companies. They also told her about the people they knew in the third company, which she was able to note for later reference.

Taken altogether, Naomi had put a networking strategy in place that neatly complemented her earlier research and provided her with a road map she could pursue in the later stages of A.I.M. She had quickly been able to determine that her best opportunities lay with the third company, allowing her to better focus her efforts. The work she had done earlier in the A.I.M. process, particularly her windowpane exercise, revealed that she was attracted to companies that were going through change. While Naomi had confided that she was tired of being in charge of making such changes happen on her own, she was open to other roles that would help a firm change. This knowledge helped us focus her research and networking strategy.

Based on her research and her initial networking contacts, Naomi put any further work with respect to the first two firms on hold and threw all of her energy into the third company. While she did not feel it was appropriate at this point to approach the firm's president, she was confident that, if she learned more about the state of the business, she could then come up with her own ideas as to what she might be able to do to help them. If she could do this, and test it with others who were closer to the company, Naomi would then feel comfortable approaching the president.

Her strategy shifted to gaining a better understanding of the internal workings of the company. Since she had pretty much exhausted the avenues of Internet and documentary research that could be conducted, Naomi instead went back to her basic research and reviewed the list of the board of directors. She then reconnected with some of those with whom she had already networked, and asked them for referrals to specific contacts on the board. Her contacts were happy to help, connecting her with one of the directors. In that meeting, she explained her curiosity about the company, her profile and strengths she could offer. The director, in turn, was so impressed with her background and the knowledge she had about the company, that he immediately connected her with the president. Within a few weeks, Naomi was working on a consulting contract to examine the strategic options for improving the company's flagging transportation business.

Naomi and I had lunch shortly after she began her consulting engagement. She was bursting to share the story of how her research and networking strategy had paid incredible dividends.

"Jim," she said, "if I had followed my instincts, I would have just plunged into looking at my options. But taking the time really paid off."

Mapping out your own networking strategy

Building on Naomi's example, it is now time for you to map out your own networking strategy. When doing so, consider the questions you might have with respect to the different areas you have identified in your future options list. Specifically, with respect to what you might want to explore, ask yourself the following question:

> Do I know someone who might be able to answer the questions I have or introduce me to people who might be able to provide the answers?

When considering this question, think about the various networks you may be able to access, but might not consciously think of right away. You might, for example, consider people you know through your current or former employers, through family or friends, and those you may know through social groups, such as sports leagues, volunteer positions, or parent groups. You can supplement this list with others you may not know directly, but think might be interesting people to speak with about your options. Such people often turn up spontaneously in your research so in these cases, make note of their names, positions, and contact information, and then add them to your list.

With each area identified under your future options list, begin writing names of people who may be able to help you explore that area further. In the following chapter, you will learn more about how you can approach these people, but for now, just capture the names of people who may be able to help you. By the end of this exercise, you should have at least three names for each of the options you would like to explore.

A simple way to keep track of your networking list is to create a basic Excel spreadsheet or mirror the following format on a piece of paper. As you will see, it can allow you to keep track of the contacts you are making and the results of any meeting you might have with them.

NETWORKING PROSPECT LIST

OPTION: Moving to another company similar to my own

NAME	TITLE	CONTACT INFO	DATE CONTACTED	RESULT	FOLLOW-UP
Marie Jones	VP, Planning	1234 New directions way, Anytown, XX, 555-1212, mjones @megacorp.com	to be filled in once you begin contacting people	to be filled in once you begin contacting people	to be filled in once you begin contacting people

Now that you have identified your initial networking contact list, put it aside. We will come back to these names once you have completed the exercises in the remaining stages of A.I.M. We will now move on to the practical tools you will need to conduct networking meetings in our chapter on "Filling Up Your Toolkit."

CHAPTER 10

Filling Up Your Toolkit

We shall not weaken or tire . . . give us the tools and
we will finish the job.

—Sir Winston Churchill

In the previous stages of the A.I.M. process, you have slowly and
methodically built your case for change. We have led you through
exercises that have helped you to identify what you value and why,
looking at the various patterns in your life and what they might say
about the choices you are *likely* to make in the future. We have used
that information to identify possible changes you want to make in
your life, as well as an outside perspective (your reality banker) and
some difficult questions to, hopefully, narrow those choices further.
In the preceding chapter, we started to answer questions you might
have about your possible choices through the use of research and
identifying people with whom you can network.

There is still one more step to complete before you can go out
into the world and make your change happen. As you may have gathered, the A.I.M. process has been designed to reduce the risk that
you may fail and increase your chances of success. The best way to
reduce the risk of failure is to find ways to prevent you from doing

what your instinct is telling you—namely, to leap into action before you develop a plan, conduct basic research, narrow your choices, and figure out how best to apply your scarce time and energy to the changes you need to make.

Once you have done all of this, however, you still need one more important asset before making your change happen in earnest. In order to talk to someone about change, you will need to know *what* to say and *how* to say it. There are several standard tools that you can use to help you convey your story in the simplest, and most powerful, way possible to the people you will meet.

Let's say you think you are ready to meet one of the people you have identified to help you explore one of your options. You telephone them, they answer, and then . . . What do you say? Someone you have never met before is on the other end of a phone line, possibly ready to help you. Are you confident that you can now tell him or her exactly who you are, why you are contacting them, and what they can do to help you?

Perhaps it isn't that cut and dried. For example, you have decided to explore a career change and are meeting with a friend who works at one of the companies you have identified as an ideal future employer. Scarcely have you settled in her office when the CEO knocks on the door and walks in.

"So good you dropped in," your friend says to her boss. "I am just meeting with a colleague of mine who is interested in working here. This is Craig, our CEO."

He holds out his hand, shakes yours, and then it hits you. Getting a meeting with the CEO might have taken you months—if you could have arranged one at all. Now he is standing in front of you, waiting for you to say something. You have twenty seconds to impress him by saying something that will sum up who you are in a way that will engage him, so he will want to talk some more with you. Instead, you mumble something general and he leaves—taking with him an excellent opportunity that you may never have again.

You get the picture. You have come too far in the A.I.M. process to risk blowing it all by beginning a series of meetings without anything to present. This chapter is about just that—ensuring that you have "tools" in your "toolkit" which you can take out and use to move your options further ahead. The three key tools we will create in this chapter are the elevator speech, a written one-page profile, and, perhaps the most misunderstood tool of all, a resumé. We will also work through how to approach your potential networking contacts and create a series of standard scripts that you can adapt when you contact them by phone or e-mail.

Your tools

People lead busy lives. Most of us work eight to ten hours a day. We then spend time with partners, families, or friends. Household chores and errands take up time, as do sporting or leisure activities, hobbies, or the general "boy, I really need to do that today" tasks that seem to fill up every spare moment. Then there are the occasional educational courses, volunteering at charities or nonprofit organizations, or your spiritual life may involve time spent in churches or other houses of worship.

Research backs up that our free time is shrinking, telling us that the average person has less and less time to complete important tasks. One thing that suffers is our sleep, as studies point out that the average person now sleeps less, but does more in their waking hours, than their parents or grandparents.

The bottom line is that, in a busy world, we all have less and less time to spend on things that might not immediately make sense to us. It is into this busy reality that you will be trying to engage people to talk about your options. While you have been thinking about the changes you would like to make for some time, and have been walking through the stages of A.I.M. for days if not weeks, those people you are planning to contact have not. They have no idea what you have been thinking about or going through. Instead, they will not have much time to size up who you are and what you are asking of them. This means that any contact you make with them has to be efficient—it has to make immediate sense and you have to make each contact count. The following three exercises are all about making your point in as logical and direct a fashion as you can.

The starting point—the elevator speech

In the previous chapter, we saw how extensive research paid off for Naomi, narrowing her search and identifying whom she should approach to learn more about her preferred option for future employment. In the various stages of Naomi's research, she needed to approach people for information and referrals, ultimately to secure interviews. What did she have to do beyond her research to make all of these contacts happen? How did she talk with people she didn't know? What did she say and why did it work?

Once you have mapped out the people you want to approach, the starting point in networking is the elevator speech. The name comes from a simple metaphor. Imagine you are standing alone in an elevator on the ground floor. Just as the doors are about to close, someone else steps in. As luck would have it, this person is someone you have always wanted to meet—someone about whom you have always thought, "Boy, if I could get a few minutes with that person it would really help." The doors close and the elevator begins to ascend. You may only have thirty seconds or perhaps a minute to connect with this person, or forever lose what could be a life-altering chance. What are you going to say that can create a memorable impression with that person, opening doors and helping you move ahead?

You need to create a basic speech that will run no more than sixty seconds that effectively says who you are, where you are coming from, where you want to go, and what the other person can do to help you. That is the essence of a good elevator speech. Your starting point should be your windowpane exercise, where you mapped the "four-dimensional you." Take that page and look at the points you made in each of the quadrants. These should sum up most, if not all, of your high points concerning your values and your professional and personal achievements. Look at this document—what are the key things you think are worth mentioning in the sixty seconds you now have to make your point?

In my coaching practice, as you may have noticed, the first question I pose to a new client is, "Tell me about yourself?" Nine out of ten clients typically answer that question with a question—a variant of "Where do you want me to start?" or "What do you want to know?" When I tell them to begin where they feel most comfortable, they usually start with their career, talking about what they are doing now, their immediate challenges, problems with their boss or their employees, and the small changes that, if realized, would make everything okay. This speech is over well before the thirty-second mark. The good news about such a speech is that I now know what is on their mind. The bad news is that these "off the top of my head" remarks never work as an effective elevator speech. Instead, they make you sound like everyone else—trapped, ordinary, and focused on the small things that really don't matter to others, or to the longer story of your life, for that matter.

As I work with clients through the early stages of the A.I.M. process, I generally help them out with questions that open up the other dimensions of who they are. I might ask them where they grew up, the schools that they attended, sports they may have enjoyed, highlights from their family life, etc. Usually, after about 30 minutes or so of such a conversation, I can "play back" to them a broad sketch of who they are in a way they usually had not thought about themselves before. In most cases, the client is shocked with how I would portray them. It is not that I am exaggerating or emphasizing those things they are not proud of—it is just that people, in general, have a huge blind spot about themselves and their achievements. Things that we do every day that would be fascinating to others we often take for granted about ourselves.

Terry O'Reilly, an international ad executive, tells a great story in his award-winning radio series, *The Age of Persuasion*, about golfer Tiger Woods that illustrates this well. As part of a promotional campaign for a car company, a colleague of O'Reilly's was planning a hidden camera ad that would see Woods walk up to unsuspecting golfers at a Florida course and challenge them to a "closest to the pin" contest, where the winner would walk away with a new SUV. When the ad company was explaining the concept to Woods, however, he was immediately concerned.

"What if they don't want to play with me?" he said. "What if they are having a great game when I ask to join them and they don't want me to ruin it?"

The ad agency staff were dumbfounded, but quickly understood that Woods was not pulling their leg. He genuinely believed someone might say "no," and he didn't realize that any golfer in the world would abandon *their* best game ever in order to play one round with him. Understandably, the filming of the ads went as planned. The golfers were all surprised and incredibly grateful to golf with Woods. But in a subsequent interview, he still seemed surprised, saying, "Wow—no one turned me down when I asked. That was nice."

Just as Tiger Woods apparently has a huge and endearing blind spot about how others might see him, so do most other people. We all have interesting aspects to our stories which others might find engaging that, for some reason, we take for granted. Finding those interesting points that accurately convey who you are in a manner that cuts through the clutter is the key to creating your own elevator speech.

Everyone has a limited attention span. Each day, we meet different people, see countless ads, visit dozens of websites, and receive countless e-mails. In all this clutter, people have only a small portion of attention to devote to anything new. So, if you are meeting someone new, they will accord you a small portion of their overall attention. In that small amount of time, you have a brief window of opportunity, so make it count.

In many ways, the elevator speech is similar to creating a good personal brand. Brands such as Nike, Gap, Apple, or Toyota "work" in a consumer environment cluttered with tens of thousands of competitors, because they stand out. They communicate things clearly in a way that is backed up by reality. Apple, for example, clearly communicates that its technology is "cool," creative, and reliable. The company doesn't need pages and pages of text to tell you that—it just needs a photo or two, a few words, and a symbol that is recognized the world over. That symbol and a few words convey distinctiveness and accurately say to consumers, "This is who I am and this is why I matter."

Ask yourself similar questions when looking at your windowpane exercise. What is distinctive or special about you that will draw the attention of someone else? What is your "story" that accurately answers: 1) who you are; 2) where you are coming from; 3) where you want to go; and 4) how the other person can help.

Paulo's story: From introvert to powerhouse

Of all the clients I have coached through the elevator speech exercise, Paulo's story offers the best example of how someone really grew through the process.

An up-and-coming financial analyst in his late thirties, Paulo worked for an international bank. He was referred to me by a former colleague in the investment field. When he settled his lanky frame into the chair opposite my desk, I immediately sensed he was nervous—a suspicion confirmed by the hesitant and guarded answers he gave to my initial questions.

When I asked him to "tell me about yourself," predictably, he answered with other questions. When I rephrased the question and asked it again, he began to expand on the technical aspects of his career. He talked in short, curt sentences about his role as an oil analyst for the bank and his concerns about what his next career step might be.

Sensing he was finally beginning to relax, I began to gently ask more probing questions about various aspects of his life. To my surprise, I learned that Paulo had led a very interesting life for someone so young. Unlike many of the other children in the immigrant enclave in which he grew up out west, he had gone to a small private school. There he had been a very promising football player who could have attended a U.S. school on a scholarship. He had decided instead to forgo the scholarship and a potential athletic career, and focused all his energy on the engineering field. During the summers, he had worked on an oil field crew, working on various parts of the drilling rig with a cast of very rugged characters, while playing his guitar for them in the evenings. Upon graduating, he joined an oil company as an engineer, but shifted into the financial industry after a few years, rising quickly to head up a bank's oil field analysis desk. Along the way, he had married and was raising two young boys. In addition to shuttling them to basketball games, the family enjoyed the outdoors.

He still found time for the occasional game of football and he continued to play the guitar for his family and friends.

After drawing all of these details out of Paulo, I played them back to him in the form of a rough narrative, ending with a few simple questions. I asked, "Don't you think that others would find this story interesting? It's not really a traditional career path for someone working in the financial industry, is it?"

He paused, sat back, and pursed his lips. "I guess not, Jim," he answered. "I've never thought of it that way before."

With this encouraging response, I continued. "Why don't we start all over again? Pretend you have just met me. Now give me a quick elevator speech about yourself based on what I have just told you."

Suddenly, the room went cold. Paulo grimaced and looked away. "I don't think I can do that, Jim," he said, "I'm just not that comfortable talking about myself."

I've often had clients who voiced the same concern. Modesty is a virtue in our society—for good reason. No one likes a self-promoting blowhard who talks about himself constantly. Instead, we value others who take an interest in us and want to learn more about all the people around them. There is a lot of room, however, between being the egotist that no one likes and being someone who is comfortable talking about himself when it is appropriate. The main problem with Paulo was that he was so modest that it might get in the way of his being able to effectively move his career to the next level. While he was not going to turn into an Obama-esque public speaker, I had to find a way to get him to be more comfortable talking about himself, before he began to meet others to explore his options.

"Here's what I am going to suggest," I began. "Why don't you go away and write up what you think others should know about you, and then we can discuss that the next time we meet."

Relieved, Paulo did just that. When we met a week or so later, he had developed what I considered an excellent first draft of an elevator speech:

My name is Paulo S. and I currently work as an investment analyst at ABC, where I specialize in the oil industry.

I learned about the industry working on an oil rig in my early twenties, and then worked in the oil patch as an engineer once I got out of university. I have been involved with some aspect of the oil industry over the past fifteen years, and now I am looking to move to the next level of my career, capitalizing on my strengths in engineering and financial analysis. Personally, I spend a lot of time with my wife and two fantastic kids. We are all active in sports and my kids have followed in my footsteps and taken up playing the guitar.

As we read this draft together, I could sense that Paulo was much more relaxed than he had been in our previous meeting. He had psychologically made the transformation from thinking he was nothing special to beginning to think about how others could see him, and how he could tell others a story that they would understand and value.

"How do you feel about this?" I asked him.

"Jim," he replied, "it was a little awkward beginning this, but I think I'm finally starting to get it. I tried this out on my wife and a friend of mine and they both thought it was great. Now what do we do?"

In a few short weeks, he had gone from someone who was reluctant to talk about himself to someone who was now ready to use this first important tool—the elevator speech—to engage others in a discussion of his options.

Writing your own elevator speech

After you have reviewed your windowpane and decade in review exercises, put them to one side. Picture, sitting opposite you, someone you have never met, but who may be able to help you with your life transition. With the points from those two exercises, write a series of sentences that will explain you to that person in a way that will interest them. Reveal relevant information and prompt them, at the end of the speech, to be more likely to understand and help you than they were before.

In doing so, consider how you could answer the following questions:

- Who are you, really?
- Where have you come from career-wise, geographically, in life, etc.?
- Building on your second point, where do you want to go now?
- What kind of help will get you there?

Review the answers you jot down and try to fashion them into a coherent story, ensuring that the total does not exceed sixty seconds in length. Try as many drafts as it takes to make it seem natural to you, then try it out on someone close to you who can offer some feedback. Once you are satisfied with it, put it aside. This elevator speech will become part of your approach in the networking phase and will serve as the basis of the basic communication you will undertake as you move forward.

Creating your one-page profile

The next tool you will develop is a one-page profile on yourself. Like the elevator speech, the one-page profile is a basic document that will assist you in explaining yourself to people who need more information. As you move through your career or life transition, there will be situations where you may want to share such a summary to highlight the key points about who you are and what you are trying to do.

The outcome is a little like the stories you might read in the newspaper every day. When teaching new journalists how to write these stories, instructors stress that the most important facts should come first, followed by supporting details that round out the story and answer any unanswered questions. In many ways, this is exactly what you would do if you were to tell a story about something unexpected that happened during your workday. If you are walking up your driveway after work and a neighbor's dog bites you, you will probably tell the first person you see, "Hey, I was just bitten by a dog."

You would not come into the house, pour yourself a glass of milk, and talk for half an hour about the weather before casually saying, "Oh, the dog next door bit me half an hour ago." The other supporting details will come later, but a news story—just like your one-page summary—is a distinct package that takes the reader from the start to the finish. With this process, the story engages a person from the outset and provides information they didn't have before. It engages them further in *your* story, with details that work with each other to provide a complete package of information.

This is the key challenge in creating your one-page profile. Within the confines of a single page—approximately 300 words—you need to convey the essence of what you want someone to know about you. It is important to remember that this is **not** a resumé, but a more extensive version of your elevator speech.

In Paulo's case, the progress he had made with the elevator speech helped in his transition to the one-page summary. In our subsequent meetings, when I introduced him to the idea of fleshing out his elevator speech into a longer document, he had a few questions about its purpose and what it should look like. Once I explained the difference between the summary and a resumé, however, he "got it" right away.

In the span of a week, here is what Paulo came back with:

Paulo S.

Objective: To use my engineering and financial skills to move to a more senior role in corporate finance for an organization in the energy field.

I have spent more than fifteen years in the oil industry and now work in an executive capacity, heading up the analysis team for ABC Bank. With my ten staff, we regularly analyze the strengths and weaknesses of major oil companies for investors.

I grew up in the west and have spent all of my life here. I went to university here and received a degree in chemical engineering. I still found time for football at university and, as a halfback, was on the 1999 team that won the national championship.

I have always enjoyed being around the oil fields. I put myself through school by working on drilling rigs during the summers. When I graduated, I joined XYZ Oil Company as an engineer and, within a few years, had become a production supervisor for their biggest plant.

In this position, I managed a team of ten junior engineers. I found my experience in team sports helped a lot, allowing me to provide leadership and practice a "lead by example" style of management.

Numbers have always interested me, and this interest in markets and company performance saw me move on to become an investment analyst with ABC Bank. In the past several years, I have risen to lead their analysis team and have developed a much stronger skill base, particularly in corporate finance.

My family and I like living in the west. My two young boys are quite active in basketball and have embraced my love of music, following in my footsteps to take up playing the guitar.

While I am happy with how far I have come, I am now thinking about the next stage of my career and where I can go to make even more of a contribution that builds on where I have come from.

I was quite pleased with what Paulo had come up with. In a little more than three hundred words, he had begun to tell a story that would engage the people he approached. From his summary, you can see he has given the reader a good glimpse into many aspects of his life. There is a little bit of the personal, professional, and comments about what is important to him and his family. Moreover, it begins to ask the question, "What is next for this guy?"—a question that many of the people he will be approaching should be able to help him with.

Paulo also made a statement about his objective upfront. You can customize this objective, depending on whom you share the document with, so getting it "right" the first time is less important. What such a statement does, however, is immediately tell the reader "here is what I am trying to do." This, in turn, serves as an important reference point as they begin reading your story.

Writing your own one-page summary
As was the case with your elevator speech, consider your window-pane and decade in review exercises. Look for how you have made progress over the years towards a goal that the reader may be able to understand. Pay particular attention to how your values and actions may fit together to form a story. Look for elements that others may respond to—much as Paulo linked football to leading a work team. Weave in personal details that are relevant to your overall story, and try to avoid any jarring details that may raise more questions than they answer. Paulo's family story was a good one, but many of us have had troubled relationships, so try to avoid anything that looks like it would interrupt a good narrative arc. Moving from university to his two work positions and a happy family worked for Paulo. If he had divorced twice and moved to get away from bad personal memories, I would have counseled him to avoid those details.

With these points in mind, take your elevator speech and expand on it. Begin with your objective, then flesh out a story that takes the reader from A to B in a simple manner that fills in the supporting details. In Paulo's story, for example, his move from an oil company to a bank was a natural progression that, in turn, leads to his final question—where to go next? Think of similar details for your story that will allow the reader to come to a conclusion without directly stating it for them.

Once you have finished your draft one-page summary, re-read it and, if possible, simplify it. Avoid technical jargon or titles that people outside your industry might not be familiar with. Try to avoid multiple clause sentences; if there are more than two commas in a sentence, reword it. When you are happy with your draft, then share it with a close friend, a partner, or a colleague you trust to get their feedback. Once you have made all your changes and feel it is finished, you are now ready to move on to the final tool for your toolkit—the resumé.

Your resumé: An anchor in any transition

Very few documents have been subject to as much attention—and as much misunderstanding—as the resumé.

The basic resumé is a simple, multi-page document that outlines your work, personal history, and possible qualifications for a future position. Its name comes from the French word meaning "to summarize," and the best resumés do just that. In just a few pages, anyone should be able to see where you work, where you live, where you went to school, and what you do outside of work that is relevant to your work performance. As such, most of us focus an inordinate amount of attention on this document when we are considering a career or life transition. "How will this look on my resumé?" is a question that often is not far away from a change process.

In 90 percent of my initial coaching sessions, the client will proudly present a piece of paper to me—their resumé —as if that document will answer any question I might possibly have about them. Even before we begin our discussions, before I determine whether they are looking for career planning help, assistance with a major life transition, or just looking for a job, people seem to feel the need to share their resumé with me. There appears to be an element of security in having that piece of paper and placing it before someone.

This is not to say that having a well-written resumé is not important—it most definitely is. However, in the context of this chapter, you should be aware that it is only one of several tools that you have in your toolkit. You will notice that your resumé is not our starting point for your toolkit—just an important element that supports the overall story you are telling.

The resumé is meant to be a factual and accurate statement of your career and education. It reflects what you have done and are doing, when and where, the organization(s) you work(ed) for, your positions, and your accomplishments. You can choose to also include such things as extracurricular activities, memberships, and other personal data. In more than thirty years working as an executive search consultant and coach, however, I have yet to find one format of resumé that should be used above all others. In fact, an entire cottage industry has sprung up to offer resumé advice, standardized templates, writing help, etc., with the aim of making your resumé stand out above all others.

While proper formatting and clear communication are important, please don't be too stressed about whether your resumé is "right." Whatever you do, there are certain basics that must be adhered to:

1. **Be honest:** All the details in your resumé should check out. Some studies have found that more than 60 percent of resumés have inaccurate information. Make sure yours is in the 40 percent that is accurate. Do not try to stretch any truths to make it just that bit more interesting. If you have a degree or diploma, state it, what discipline it is in, from which institution, and the date you received the degree. If you have an incomplete degree, say so—don't bluff it. Make sure your employment dates are accurate and, if there are gaps, be prepared to explain them.

2. **Show what your employers do and what your job was:** Most of us think that, because we spend several years at XYZ Company, everyone should know what that company does and, if we include a title we have proudly borne, everyone should know what that entails. Guess again. Include a sentence after the name of each employer that explains what that company does or include it after your position title. For example:

   System Manager, XYZ Corporation, 2007–2010
   Oversaw a twelve-person team as part of XYZ's efforts to become the largest IT consulting company in the country.

3. **State your position title accurately:** While you may have been the acting divisional manager, if they didn't officially give you the title, don't include it. All it takes is one call to check your details to have a former co-worker say, "Oh, she wasn't really the acting manager," and your chances for a new position take a nosedive.

4. **Briefly describe your responsibilities:** In a few sentences or bullet points following your position description, flesh out exactly what it was you did.

5. **List accomplishments, if appropriate:** At some point in your resumé, you may want to list some of the things you have accomplished in bullet form. Again, choose wisely. For example, if you were awarded a Rhodes Scholarship and then worked overseas for a charity, that paints a compelling story. However, if you won an entrance scholarship to MIT but dropped out after only a year, you may not want to highlight that detail.

6. **Share only relevant personal data, if you want to:** Whether you want to share personal information is up to you. Should you choose to do so, make sure it fits into your overall narrative and doesn't raise questions or paint an unintended stereotype.

In all of these points, think about the story you are telling and try to avoid information that could lead a reader to either jump to conclusions or wonder why some points are seemingly at odds with one another. I once had a client, for example, who had grown up in challenging economic circumstances, but had been able to learn how to ride horses through a community program. By including his equestrian awards in his resumé, he could leave readers to assume that he had grown up in a life of privilege. Similarly, another client had noted that she had won a prestigious entrance scholarship to a technical university, only to drop out two years later and take up a completely different path. While the information was true, she may have wanted to omit the scholarship, as it may have led readers to assume she had squandered a chance that others would have been very grateful to have had.

Career objective—or not?

As we saw from Paulo's one-page summary, he included an objective at the top of his document. Many resumé "experts" recommend including such an objective at the top of every resumé and customizing them for each position you are applying for or each person with whom you share the document.

While the format you choose is up to you, I recommend to clients that they not include such statements at the top of their resumé. They have become so common that I believe they are losing any impact they might have had. So many people now customize these descriptions for the position in question that they, more often than not, appear insincere. Moreover, while I think you should absolutely customize your elevator speech and one-page profile to suit your audience, I believe you should treat your resumé as a stock item that details your actual employment and academic background. My suggestion is, if you want to talk about your career objectives, put them in your cover letter where you can place them into a better context than including them alongside your actual work and academic history.

Opening your toolkit and beginning to network

We now have a well-equipped toolkit that will allow you to talk about yourself and provide a persuasive story about who you are, where you have come from, and where you want to go. Now it is time for us to return to the concept of **networking** in more detail.

In the last chapter, we outlined how Naomi had identified whom she wanted to contact and then approached them using information from her research to learn more about her preferred option. While identifying *whom* to approach is crucial, knowing *how* to approach someone and *what* to say once you meet with them are equally important. The techniques you use can transform a list of people you would like to share some time with into a series of meetings that will give you the information you require to move forward.

Before we start, it is important to clarify that networking is not an alien concept. The next time you are in a coffee shop or similar location during the day, look around. Chances are, if you wait long enough, you will see two people meet, introduce themselves, shake hands, and have a conversation over coffee. Perhaps they will exchange business cards or written material. Networking meetings just like this happen around the world every day.

Invariably, when I introduce clients to the concept for the first time, some will balk at the idea of networking. When I explore their opposition, it generally comes down to a feeling of disbelief that there are actually people who would respond favorably to someone contacting them out of the blue and asking to meet. As one client said to me, "Surely, Jim, these people don't just agree to meet with someone like me when I call them up. It can't be that easy?"

Well, basically, yes. There are tips and tricks that we will share in the following pages, and proper etiquette about how these meetings should progress, but it can be that easy. The work you have done in the early stages of A.I.M. ensures that you are focused and will convey a sense of purpose to those people you contact. In addition, your research and networking list should ensure that you are contacting individuals who are quite likely to help you. The type of person who can help you answer the questions about your career or life change will be familiar with the concept of networking and will make time to meet people they don't know. They realize that if they actively meet others from different walks of life, the resulting network becomes a valuable asset for them as well.

My co-writer, Alex, is a good example of someone who knows and understands the value of developing a healthy network. Despite running a busy consulting practice, teaching at a university, and writing articles and books like this one, he makes time to meet with three to five new contacts each month. At this stage of his career, most of the people he meets are referred to him by others in his network. The people who seek him out generally want advice on one of the areas in which he works—the nonprofit world, corporate citizenship, the environment—and he is generally happy to oblige.

When I introduced him to the A.I.M. concept, he was in his twenties and was skeptical. Beginning in those early days, he met with people who could help him with his transition, but now he has made networking a part of his regular schedule and orientation towards his work. Recently, he confided to me that an intern working in his office had updated his networking contact database for him, and after more than a dozen years of meeting various people, Alex now has more than 2,000 contacts.

There are millions of people around the world like Alex and myself—people who regularly practice strategic networking and welcome the opportunity to help others. From your networking research, you have probably identified a variety of contacts drawn from different networks that most people have. One of the first places that people look for contacts when drawing up their network list are those who are closest to them, followed in decreasing order by those with whom you have the closest contact. Following from this logic, there are three different types of contact you will make which should fit into one of the sections of the diagram below. Each of these contacts will require a slightly different approach, which are outlined in the following paragraphs.

Three Types of Networking Contacts

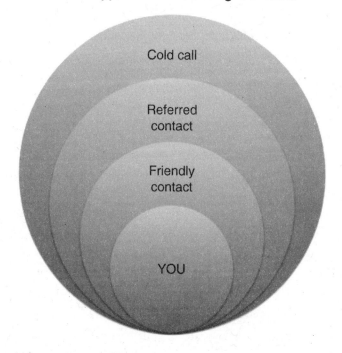

Cold call

Referred contact

Friendly contact

YOU

The friendly contact

The first people we think of when looking for help or perspective are those closest to us. Family, friends, colleagues, and former close contacts are a good place to start, if they have specific knowledge of the options you are exploring. They already know you, and asking someone for help when you already have some form of relationship with them should be easier than asking a complete stranger. You may find, like Naomi and Henry, that you already have direct contacts in the areas you want to explore. On the surface, the familiarity you have with a person should make the contact easier, but don't assume it will be a breeze. You still have to prepare as rigorously as if you were meeting someone completely new.

The following is an example of what a phone call to a friendly contact might sound like:

> "Hi, Bob. How are things going? It's been a while since we last talked, but I am calling to ask for your help. Things are going well with me, but I am at a point where I would like to get your feedback on a career/life change I am thinking about. You know me well and I respect your opinion, so I would really appreciate the opportunity to chat and get your perspective. When can we get together?"

The referred contact

Invariably, someone with whom you meet will offer to connect you with another person they think can help you to explore your options. Generally, this will happen spontaneously, but it can also happen in response to a direct request, as we will see when we explore the steps of a meeting in just a few pages. Regardless of how it happens, treat it as luck—you have met with someone who has heard your story and now wants to introduce you to someone they know who might be able to help you. These contacts are very valuable for two reasons. First, you will be meeting with someone you don't already know, thus increasing the reach of your personal network. Second, you are being introduced to this new contact by someone that person knows, making them all the more likely to meet with you and appreciate what you have to say.

You may also use an existing contact to reach one you do not know as you move through the process. It is quite possible that, after you have done a series of networking meetings, you will identify a key possible contact that you do not know, but one of your previous contacts does know. In such a case, your approach to the person you had previously met might sound like this:

> "Hi, Bob! When we met a while ago to discuss my career change, I mentioned that I was interested in the pharmaceutical industry. Someone else I recently met with said I should talk with Andre at LMNO Company, and I believe you might know him? I'm wondering if you would mind either introducing me to him with a quick e-mail or phone call, or if I could use your name when I contact him?"

Then, armed with their introduction or permission to use their name, you can reach out to the referred contact. The following is an example of what a phone call to such a contact might sound like:

> "Hi there. My name is Joan Smith. Bob Langlois suggested I give you a call. I met with him to get his input on a career change I am considering making into the pharmaceutical industry. We talked for a while and he strongly recommended that I speak with you as well. I'd like to meet with you or buy you a coffee and get your feedback if I can. I was wondering if we might meet next Thursday or the following Monday? Does one of those dates work for you?"

You will note a few differences in this call from when you were approaching a friendly contact. First of all, you should be as specific as you can about the subject of the meeting. Instead of saying, "I am exploring a life or career change," I would recommend you name the exact area you want to talk about, such as, "I met with Darlene to get her input on a career in sports management." That way, the person you are interviewing knows exactly why you want to meet with them. My clients have also found that, if you keep things general, people are less likely to make the time to meet with you. That's understandable. If someone you don't know calls you up and says,

"Hi, I want to talk to you about my life," you might think, "Wow, this person could be flaky. Do I want to take the time to meet with them?" Whereas, if the topic is specific, they should be more likely to agree to the meeting, thinking, "Well, I do know a lot about sports management, so why not?"

The script also uses a tried and true technique from marketing. It gives the contact two options for a meeting and asks them to choose, rather than asking them the open-ended question, "Do you have time to meet?" People are far more likely to either choose one of the two options or come back with a time that works for them: "Well, neither of those dates and times work for me. How is next Thursday at 10 a.m. for you?"

The "cold call" contact

The most challenging call you will have to make is what marketers call a "cold call." The name, as you may guess, comes from the fact that the contact may not be "warm" to your overture—you don't know them, and you haven't been referred to them by someone they know. As you might expect, if you don't approach them the right way, their initial response to your request may be short and negative. They are being contacted, out of the blue, by someone they don't know who is asking them to give up some of their precious time for a meeting. While this may be a challenge, it is an unavoidable one if you truly want to fully explore the areas you have identified on your future options list. If you do not have a friendly or referred contact with the information you need, you will have to dig deep and approach people who may not, initially, want to talk with you.

The good news is that the work you have done so far in the A.I.M. process, plus the judicious use of the scripts provided in this phase, should increase the odds that the cold contact will respond to your request. In your research phase, for example, you should have learned everything you can possibly find out about the organization. Let's assume that you are looking for a contact at ABC Company, because, like Naomi, you have identified that company as a potential employer for you. Before you even contact them, you should have already amassed a file with solid background information on the firm, its structure, financial performance, the bios of its key executives, how it has been covered in the business press, etc. You have, most likely, also asked people in your growing network what they know about the firm to gain their perspective. You now have to determine whom you should contact, how to contact them, what you should say, and what expectations you should set both for yourself and for them.

Whom to contact?

When approaching an organization where you do not know anyone, its size will help determine whom you can target. If the organization is a smaller firm run by a single person, you can likely target the owner. In the case of a larger company, you might start with the head of human resources or the head of a division that piques your interest. In either case, you should be able to determine from your research the name and title of the person you want to reach—having that information will greatly increase the likelihood of success. Even if you don't have this information, however, start with the switchboard and ask to be connected to the head of the department you have identified.

How to contact?

Once you have determined whom you are targeting, consider the best way to reach them. Phone calls, while nerve wracking, are often the best way to start. You can increase your chances of success by pairing a phone call with an e-mail, for example, provided you can find their contact information. Using both methods allows you to reference one contact with the other, and adds a bit of pressure to the person to respond somehow. A phone message that outlines what you want, as per the script below, can also say you will drop them an e-mail as well. This allows you to make your point twice and give the contact two ways to respond, either through a return call or by return e-mail. The use of an e-mail also allows you to follow up a week or so later if you have not heard back from them, to give a gentle reminder that you are interested in meeting with them.

What to say?

This is where wording is very important, because the cold contact will base his or her decision on whether to meet you based on just one source of information—what you say or write to them. They do not have a long history with you, as is the case with your friendly contact, nor has someone they know vouched for you, as in the case of the referral. Your words will say it all here, so pay careful attention to them.

Here is an example of what a cold call might sound like:

> "Hi there. My name is Darlene Reynolds and we don't know each other. The reason for my call is that I am currently the senior manager for accounts at ABC Incorporated. While I enjoy what I am doing, I am currently exploring my career options through a series of interviews with senior people in your field. I have conducted extensive research on your organization and was very impressed by the work your firm is doing in the environmental area. I would like the opportunity to meet with you briefly to discuss your history with the company and any advice you would give to someone like me, at this stage in my search. I know you have a busy schedule so I can work around that. When might you have time to meet?"

You will notice that this script accomplishes several strategic points. It establishes that you are coming from a legitimate position (senior manager for accounts at ABC Incorporated), telling the prospect that you are not just someone who found his or her name in the phone book. It flatters the prospect a little, by inferring that he or she is a "senior person" in the field. It tells them that you are interested enough in their firm to have conducted research on it. It acknowledges one of their probable objections to meeting, "I'm too busy," by saying you can work around their schedule. Most importantly, it does not ask the person for a job. Instead, it positions you as asking for advice about a field in which the prospect should be an expert. If you land the meeting, you can always ask them about employment opportunities in their firm at the end of the meeting, but for now, you are trying not to scare them off.

This phone script can easily be adapted for either an e-mail or a voice-mail message. If you choose to use the script in that manner, be sure you leave contact details so the person can get back to you, such as a phone number that they, or their assistant, can use to return your call. If you choose to e-mail them, you also have a one-page profile and/or a resumé that you can send as well, to increase the chances they will say "yes."

What to expect

Given that the prospect does not know you, and you have little information on which to judge whether your story may resonate with him or her, don't expect that every cold contact will immediately call or e-mail you back to book a meeting. Cold calls are named that for a reason—that is the reception you often receive. They can be incredibly valuable, however, for two reasons. First, they connect you to people completely outside of your normal network. Second, over time, they also build your confidence—even if you face continual rejection. You may be a person who, at the start of this process, would never have called someone you did not know. After a few weeks of cold calling, however, you may view cold calling as normal, and be able to use it again and again as you move forward in your career.

If nothing comes from your specific cold contact, don't become distressed. Be sure to keep track of his or her information and move on to your other contacts. You may uncover other connections down the road that will be able to open up a new channel to reach that person.

Tips and techniques: The in-person meeting

By pursuing any type of networking contacts, you will eventually begin to generate face-to-face meetings. Any of these meetings could hold the key for you to obtain the goal you have set for yourself, so take them seriously. There are common expectations for such meetings, and you would be well advised to follow that protocol to ensure they are as productive as possible.

Protocol for every meeting:

1. **Be on time. No exceptions.** I once arrived for a meeting 2 minutes late with an executive at a Swiss bank. The meeting

did not go well, as my contact was a busy woman who did not like to waste her time. I was completely at fault and, since that time, I make sure I am not late for such meetings. As a fallback, I always note the cell or BlackBerry number for my contact when I set up a meeting, in the unlikely event that I am stuck in traffic and need to let the person know that I am running late.

2. **Dress appropriately.** We often overlook how we dress and focus instead on the wordsmithery of our resumé or doing last-minute research. Yet research tells us that people make up their minds about others within seconds of meeting them, and those initial impressions are very difficult to change. This means that personal appearance matters, like it or not. If you are meeting at an organization you have never been to, try to visit the area a few days in advance and observe the people going into the building to see how they are dressed. Your contact may have a photo or two on the Internet, so you may want to search for them using the Google "image" search to see how they might normally dress. In any case, be neat, tidy, and, if there is any doubt, it is better to overdress. You can always take off a tie or drape a jacket over a chair if you feel you have missed the mark by dressing up, but it's hard to dress up from a down position.

3. **Make eye contact** with the person at the start of the meeting, especially as you shake his or her hand. Continue this practice during the meeting, using eye contact to make key points or to reinforce your interest when your contact is talking. If you feel you have to make a very important point, borrow a technique from Hollywood—keep your head perfectly still, eyes locked on the other person, finishing with a smile to show you are not trying to intimidate them. During the meeting, be sure you don't take this approach too far and end up staring or glaring at the person. Also, you should make sure to keep your head up—looking at the floor is a good way to lose your audience.

4. **Time check.** Ask the person how much time they have at the start of the meeting. A friendly, "Glad you could make the

time today. When do you have to be back at the office or at your next destination?" should suffice. This gives your contact the opportunity to set boundaries.

5. **State your purpose.** At the start of the meeting, reinforce how you came to meet the person and what the purpose is of the meeting. Don't assume the person will remember all the details of your initial phone call or e-mail exchange, so gently remind him or her. This could be as simple as referencing the person who connected you, noting how you know that person and then moving on to the purpose of the meeting. For example, "I'm glad Bernadette suggested that I call you. I've known her since university and I really trust her advice. When I was explaining to her that I wanted to explore jobs in the pharmaceutical industry, she suggested that I should call you."

6. **Give the elevator speech.** After you have established the protocol for the meeting (length of time, why you are there), give your elevator speech. Usually when people do this, they make one of three mistakes:

    i) Assume that they are very interesting to the person they are meeting, and going on about themselves for too long;

    ii) Assume that the person won't be interested in them and cutting their details short; and

    iii) Give their speech, but then continuing to talk, not giving their contact the time to respond (see Step 7 below). Be conscious of these common mistakes—and don't make them.

7. **When your speech is done, stop talking and listen.** My co-author, Alex, has a colleague who is a top fundraiser for a large charity. He has a golden rule—once you state the amount of money you want from a donor, stop talking and listen. It is human nature to be a little nervous and to hide your anxiety by talking. Don't. Once you have delivered your speech, listen.

8. **Use the conversation to get your questions out.** Once you have delivered your speech, your contact will probably ask a

few questions for clarification and, if things are going well, these will lead into a conversation. Be sure to work the questions you want answered into the conversation. Take notes if you have to, but remember that you arranged this meeting for a purpose—to gather information about the option you identified in your future options list. Be sure you do that.

9. **Say thanks and then ask for help.** There are two words that every child and networker should learn—thank you. A sincere "thank you" at the end of a meeting is icing on the cake. It acknowledges that the person you have met really didn't have to meet you—they did it as a favor. Therefore, be sure to say thanks. And while you are thanking them, ask them for one more favor, but be sure to work it in as part of the close of the meeting. Ask them if there is anyone they think you should meet as you continue your search. This could be as simple as the following:

> "Janine, I want to thank you for taking the time to meet with me today. I know you're a busy person, so I appreciate being able to talk with you. Now that you've heard about what I'm doing, is there anyone else you know that you think I should talk with?"

10. **Close with a promise.** Now that someone has spent their valuable time to help you, you need to commit to keep them in the loop. As the meeting is concluding and you are saying your thanks, be sure to let them know you will keep them informed as your search progresses. This serves three purposes: 1) it is common courtesy; 2) it allows you to come back to them if you uncover more information that you think they may be able to help you with; and 3) it opens a channel for you to keep in touch with them as you move forward, hopefully making them a part of your permanent network.

11. **Write them a note.** In addition to a verbal "thank you," I have always thought it is good practice to drop a card or a handwritten note in the mail to your contact, thanking them again and making an offer to help them if there is anything you can do for them.

From questions to a conversation: When a meeting goes well
Many of my clients are anxious about their first foray into networking.
Some have asked, "But how will I know if it is going well?" The answer
is simple. Human beings do not communicate through scripts; they
have conversations. The guidelines that we have just reviewed are
just that—guidelines. They should help you start what should then
become a natural conversation, where you trade ideas and information in a friendly and professional manner. You probably won't notice
this until after the meeting is over, but at some point, the awkwardness will fade and you will find yourself having a conversation with
a person you didn't really know all that well.

I recently reconnected with someone I had helped a few years
ago, and her progress serves as a great example of how someone
can reach a level of sophistication and comfort with networking in
a relatively short period of time.

When I met Natalia, she was a vice president of planning at a major
financial institution. Another coach that I had known for years suggested
she meet with me, as I have worked with dozens of banks and insurance
companies in my career and, consequently, have a well-developed
network in this area. As a senior executive, Natalia was already familiar
with most of the networking concepts that form the basis of the A.I.M.
process, so I expected a fairly standard meeting where I would learn
more about her challenges and see if I could help her out.

We first met in a downtown coffee shop around the corner from
my office. I was early, but she was 10 minutes late. The meeting went
fairly well. While she was pleasant, courteous, and polite, I could tell
that she was new to networking and could probably use a few point-
ers. I learned from her elevator speech that she was enjoying her
position as a VP, but was in the early stages of exploring her options.
She asked a few awkward questions, but after 10 minutes or so of my
gentle questioning and reassurances, she began to relax. The meeting
then became a lot more productive, and I was able to offer her some
suggestions, not only to improve her approach to people like me,
but to her overall task of exploring her options in the financial field.

Our discussion moved on to the issues facing her industry, and
I found her to be a very strategic thinker who was very well versed

in the financial services environment. Our meeting closed with a handshake and a promise on my part to introduce her to a few contacts in other large financial firms. In the coming weeks I did just that, and she moved on to continue her search.

Then, a few years ago, Natalia got back in touch with me. I met her in the same coffee shop where we had first met four years before. I was early, but she was already waiting there for me. This time, there was no awkwardness, just a poised and confident professional who shared her challenges with me and took the time to really listen to what I was saying. She explained that one of the contacts I had connected her with had eventually offered her a long-term contract, which she had just completed.

"I should have called or written to thank you for that, Jim," she said, "but I wasn't as organized then as I am now."

Our conversation continued and, pleased with the progress she had made, I offered to connect her with additional contacts to help with her current search. We parted again with a handshake and by the time I returned to my office there was already an e-mail from Natalia waiting to thank me for the meeting. In the following months, she continued to drop me the occasional e-mail and phone call, asking advice and keeping me posted on her progress, eventually sharing that she had accepted a new position as a key advisor to a CEO. She now asks me for coffee a few times a year and has even begun to suggest people from her growing network that I should talk with about some projects that I am working on. In just a few years, she has moved from being a well-intentioned but slightly awkward networker, to a practiced professional who now helps others as much as they once helped her.

This idea of living the A.I.M. process, of making your career and life more resilient by putting A.I.M. into constant practice, is the key point behind our remaining stages. Throughout this stage, we have filled up your toolkit. We have developed the standard tools that will equip you to go out and begin to engage others in your career or life transition. In the next stage, "NET Growth: Networking, Exploring, Transforming," we will look at how you can continually improve and assess your results as you move forward.

CHAPTER 11

NET Growth: Networking, Exploring, Transforming

Do not have an opinion while you listen because frankly, your opinion doesn't hold much water outside of Your Universe. Just listen. Listen until their brain has been twisted like a dripping towel and what they have to say is all over the floor.

—Hugh Elliott

Change is a constant presence in all of our lives. The A.I.M. process is founded on the idea that we live in a constantly changing environment, that often either surprises us with the unexpected or simply sidelines us with situations that we would not have rationally chosen. Around the world, perfectly reasonable, intelligent people with solid potential to take charge of their lives, to succeed, and to give back to their fellow citizens often find themselves in situations that stifle their creativity and leave them with the vague, yet growing, feelings that they could do better.

The A.I.M. process that we have been working our way through began with the realization that better *is* possible. The end goal of the process is to allow you to make changes happen and not be a victim of circumstance; to reach a point where you have proactively identified what it is you want to do and are actively working to make that happen each and every day. When, in the first stage of the A.I.M. process, you "faced the hard truth" and asked yourself some serious questions about your current situation, you began a journey to explore not just the areas you identified in your future options list, but also to transition to a new way of living that put you on a path that fits best with your values, your past, and focused you on becoming the engaged, self-determined person you know you can be.

Since beginning this journey, you have completed the following eight stages:

1. When you began by **facing the hard truth**, you asked some difficult questions about why you were unhappy and whether you were prepared to undertake the A.I.M. process. You then developed your statement of focus that broadly defined what you were trying to change.

2. When you mapped the **four-dimensional you**, you conducted a windowpane exercise to map the different dimensions of what you valued. You also conducted a **decade review** exercise to identify patterns from your past and how they may have shaped decisions you are currently making.

3. By **sketching success**, you explored your strengths and weaknesses with respect to your broad goals and then developed a future options list of areas you would like to explore through the process.

4. In the fourth stage, you paused to **review what's important**. You looked at all of your previous exercises and began to weave them into a story that you could fine tune and then discuss with close confidants.

5. Having laid a foundation with some focused exercises, you then turned to those around you to **cash a reality check**, testing your ideas about what types of change you might want to explore.

6. With this feedback, you then looked at your options again and **asked some hard questions**, performing an exercise that looked at the feasibility of some of your choices in the harsh light of day.

7. With your general directions now set, you began **road mapping** your directions, conducting research on your possible choices, and then identifying the beginning of a networking list of contacts to help you explore them.

8. Finally, you took the time to fill up your **toolkit** for networking, giving you the scripts and skills necessary to begin engaging people about your options and how you might pursue them.

We have made significant progress as we have traveled through these eight stages of the A.I.M. process. Two more stages remain—"NET Growth: Networking, Exploring, Transforming" and "A.I.M. in Constant Motion." These two final stages are crucial to realizing your goals *and* to making sure you are prepared to handle future challenges in ways you never could have thought possible.

In this current chapter, our main priority will be to greatly expand your networking efforts to explore the areas you have identified in your future options list, so you will be able to bring about some form of change with respect to these options. This has been our goal since we began the process—to ensure that you achieve, to your satisfaction, some measure of success with respect to them. In the final stage, which is covered in the subsequent chapter, we look at how you can make A.I.M. a part of your everyday actions, ensuring that your life and career are resilient enough to allow you to help those around you, through your example and your actions, to begin their own journey of self-discovery. Through both of these stages, you will begin to see A.I.M. for what it can be—the foundation of an approach to life that can make you, in both the short and long term, happier, more productive, and able to make a positive contribution to the lives of those around you.

Let us now turn our attention to how you can greatly expand your initial networking efforts to achieve the goals you set out to attain with respect to your career or life change.

Mark's cautionary tale: Declaring victory too early

There is one issue I have seen emerge repeatedly at this stage of the A.I.M. process. A client who has done very disciplined work over the course of weeks or months will, in their first few forays into networking, find what they think is a promising opportunity and jump at it. By declaring victory too soon, they often abandon other promising leads and fail to fully integrate the changes that A.I.M. can truly make to the way they approach their life and career. I am always disappointed when I see a client who has invested considerable time and effort in the first few stages of the A.I.M. process, and then abandon it when they begin to get positive responses to their initial networking.

I can think of no better example of this from my decades of coaching than Mark, a client who seemed to have understood the intent of A.I.M. and made remarkable progress through its early stages, but almost wasted his time and effort just as the process was about to reach its conclusion.

I met Mark for the first time on a sunny afternoon in my downtown office. He worked as the chief information officer for a large municipality, where he managed a department of hundreds of employees that met the data needs of dozens of city departments. He had been referred to me by Mohammed, another executive I had coached previously, who had talked with Mark about the huge benefit he had received from working through the A.I.M. method, suggesting it might be a good fit for Mark. As he settled into the chair opposite my desk as so many other clients had done in the past, I sensed that there was something a little different about this client. Aside from exuding a tremendous amount of nervous energy, Mark was carrying a three-ring binder that appeared to be stuffed with paper.

Without taking a breath, Mark explained that he had been offered a very generous early retirement package as part of an organizational restructuring process. He knew the offer was too good to turn down, so he viewed it as an opportunity to make a significant life change which, at only fifty-four, he was still young enough to take advantage of.

"Jim," he said, leaning forward in his chair, "this could be really good for me. I just want to make sure that I get it right."

"Well, Mark," I replied, "that is what the A.I.M. method is intended to do. So why don't you tell me about . . ."

Before I could even finish my traditional starting question, he was already ahead of me, excitedly opening his binder and taking out various papers to spread across my desk.

"Yes . . . I know all about A.I.M. Mohammed told me about the basics so I got started on it last week. Here is my focus statement, my windowpane, and the decade in review," he said excitedly, jabbing his finger at the papers now covering my desk. "And here are the areas I would like to explore and some people I think I should talk with first!" He then laid out what looked like the beginnings of a rough toolkit, including a new copy of his resumé and samples of his previous work.

To say I was a little taken aback would be an understatement. With little or no understanding of the method other than a brief outline from my former client (and with far less-detailed information than we have reviewed in this book), he had tried to complete the process on his own and was now looking for me to validate his work.

After laying it all out for me and explaining each element, he concluded with, "So, who do you think I should meet first?"

In less than 20 minutes, Mark had tried to show me that he had completed stages one through eight of A.I.M. and was now ready to network. Taking a deep breath, I smiled at him and, gathering up the flurry of paper that was now spread across my desk, I started to try to put him on track.

"Mark, this is great stuff," I said, tapping the pile of paper. "You have done a lot of work that will help with the process, but I would like to start with one question."

"Yes, Jim?" he leaned in to catch what I was about to say.

"Tell me about yourself," I replied, "and we will get to this just a bit down the road."

He started to reply quickly, looking puzzled, but thought the better of it. Then we started at the beginning and talked for two hours about his challenges, his past, and some of the things he wanted to do. Whenever he tried to take a paper from the pile and say, "But it's all right here," I stopped him, gently, saying, "We will get to that, but I want to hear it from you first."

In retrospect, I should have taken that first meeting as a caution that Mark was more predisposed to jump ahead in the process than any other client I had worked with. To an extent, I did change my approach somewhat, reining him back in during our next two meetings when he wanted to move on quickly without doing sufficient work with his windowpane exercise and skimming through a discussion about his decade in review. Even though he had done some good work in his initial draft, Mark found that as we discussed the various things he had identified, he began to add and improve his thoughts. At the end of our third session, he even recommitted to the process, noting that he had a once-in-a-lifetime opportunity with his severance to take the time to explore what would make him happy in the next stage of his life.

As he jotted things down and began to become excited with what he was learning about himself, I permitted myself the unwise luxury of thinking that I had gotten him back on track and he would now benefit from the A.I.M. stages as others had before him. This feeling of comfort lasted only until the end of our second meeting when, as he was packing up his papers to leave, he casually let me know that he had already booked a networking meeting "about a potential job" for the following week. In my experience with clients, I call this a "by the way" comment. If you don't pay attention to them, you are often giving them tacit approval.

"Let's just talk about this for a moment," I said. "Tell me more about this meeting."

"Well, Jim," he explained, keeping his matter-of-fact tone, "in my future options list which I showed you in our first meeting, I had identified a consulting assignment as a possible area to explore. And as luck would have it, I know someone who has a very interesting project that fits in with my skills. It's with a government agency that is working in Africa. They need someone who knows a lot about electronic data storage. I love this kind of work and it would get me up and running, as well as give me an opportunity to travel and do some good in the world."

This sounded interesting, but I was justifiably cautious. "Is this an interview, Mark? Do you think you are ready to move that quickly into a new job? I thought you wanted to take things slowly and lay the groundwork for a long-term change in your life."

"It's not really an interview, Jim—it's more like a briefing session. It might lead to an interview down the road, but I think it's too good an opportunity to pass up, so I'm going to do it."

After he left, I looked out of my office window at the skyline and the traffic below, and thought about Mark's matter-of-fact revelation. The A.I.M. process is by no means inflexible, and I firmly believed that clients should be able to take advantage of opportunities that may come out of nowhere, such as Mark's chance at a consulting assignment in Africa. My gut was telling me, however, that this was too much, too quickly. Mark was sending two very contradictory messages to me about his commitment to the process. On the one hand, he had told me that he wanted to make the best decisions he could and use the discipline and detail of the process to take the time to explore his options. On the other hand, he thought that because he had written down answers for every stage of the A.I.M. process in a matter of days, he could just speed ahead and begin holding meetings that could change his life. His reassurances that this upcoming meeting was not an interview rang hollow to me. If the discussion were to go well, would Mark be able to evaluate this opportunity in terms of others he was exploring? Would he be able to rationalize his choice and feel comfortable with it down the road, knowing that it fit well with his values, his overall direction, and his options?

Instead, it looked like he was jumping into one of the first opportunities that had come along without first using the A.I.M. process to identify what might make him happy, considering and narrowing his options, and then exploring them in depth to ensure he would be comfortable with the decision.

While Mark presented perhaps the most extreme example of someone jumping ahead in the process, he was certainly not the first client I had who had moved to the end a little too early. The one thing I had learned through past experience was sometimes you have to let people try what they feel is best, so they can learn from their mistakes. With this in mind, I closed my file on Mark and waited for our next meeting.

As it turned out, I didn't have to wait a few weeks to see Mark; he called me three days later. His "briefing" meeting with the Africa team had gone very well and they had immediately begun talking about how they could integrate him into their project. His mind was now full of questions that he could have resolved through the A.I.M. process. If he became a consultant, how would he set up a business? What should he charge? If he had to travel away from his family for weeks or months at a time, could he handle that?

I tried to provide Mark with some practical advice on his questions, suggesting a few people he might want to speak with who had done similar work in the past.

"But Jim, what can I say when I approach these guys? Are you sure they would want to help me?"

I bit my tongue and focused instead on the positive. "Mark," I advised, "you're ahead of yourself in the process, but now that you have opened this up, you've just got to roll through this one as best you can. We can connect after your next meeting with them, as you have to determine fairly quickly whether this is the opportunity you want to pursue."

At our next meeting, it was a very different Mark who came into my office. While he still carried his binder, there was disappointment written all over his face. Something had not gone well with his new venture, and after I coaxed him a little, it all came out.

"Jim, there were a lot more uncertainties with this project than I thought. Our next meeting went well, but there are now a lot of problems with their financing and they don't think they will be able to pull the project off. I thought this would be a cool thing to do and have told so many people about the possibility. I'm so disappointed and feel a little foolish for getting excited so quickly."

I commiserated with Mark and used the opportunity to direct his attention back to the process. "You will get to a point where you will find many opportunities that are just as interesting and, when you do, you will be able to evaluate them and make the right choice for you. But that will take some time. Can I count on you to work with me through this?"

Mark agreed, and in the months that followed, he became a disciplined follower of the A.I.M. process. After taking the time to learn more about his values and motivations by truly working through the early stages of the process, he then moved on to develop a new and extensive network around his options. Together, this work led to a very smooth career transition in the following months. After identifying several valid options and meeting dozens of new people as he expanded his network, he uncovered another promising consulting opportunity. He now consults regularly for his former employer and also for a range of cities across North America. His enthusiasm for his new direction is now tempered by a bit more self-knowledge. Through the A.I.M. process Mark has a healthy respect that change happens best when you have laid the groundwork for it.

How you can make it happen: Networking, exploring, and transforming

We are now moving into the phase of A.I.M. where you will undertake some serious networking to explore the areas you have identified in your future options list.

This networking will take two paths. You will begin by holding the initial meetings with the people you identified as part of your research. Then you will grow beyond these meetings, to engage a much broader and more diverse group of people that you will have uncovered through the techniques we will outline in the following pages. This second stage is incredibly important, because if you practice these techniques frequently enough and with increasing skill, you can transform not only your search for a new career or life, you can transform how you respond to life's challenges from this point forward.

A word about the long-term importance of networks

We are about to engage in networking with the specific goal of helping you explore the areas identified in your future options list, but there is a long-term importance to networking that few people are conscious of.

Robert Putnam is a professor at Harvard University who studies why some communities and societies do well in times of stress while others crumble. His research has shown that communities that have dense, overlapping social networks—what he calls "social capital"—are those that have the better outcomes for their citizens. The standard of living in such communities is higher, literacy levels are higher, a greater percentage of people vote in elections, participate in politics, and volunteer for local community organizations. Other studies have demonstrated that what is true for a community as a whole is true for individuals. The people who are most likely to be resilient in times of stress and change are those who have strong social networks.

The best way to describe these networks is that they act like shock absorbers. If you have very few networks and are suddenly faced with a serious challenge such as illness, family difficulties, or losing your job, you have a limited number of resources that you can call upon to help you. If you lose your job, for example, and have only a few networks, the number of people you can call on to say, "Hey, I'm now looking for a new job. Do you know anyone who I should talk with?" is much more limited than if you have dozens of such networks.

The conclusion to be drawn from such research is simple. Networks make communities more resilient and able to adapt to change, and they perform a similar function for individuals.

Stage one: Conduct your initial meetings

Let's turn our attention first to the networking contacts you have already identified. Through the research you conducted in the road mapping stage, you have identified your initial number of potential contacts to whom you will reach out. The toolkit phase of A.I.M. has given you scripts and materials that should increase the chance that those meetings will lead to successful outcomes.

Your first step, therefore, is to go ahead and begin making those approaches, holding those meetings, and learning what you can. What you are looking for here is, of course, largely goal-specific. If you are exploring the possibility of a career change and have identified a company you want to make contact with—such as Naomi did—then your interviews should focus on learning as much about that prospective firm as possible. You can then try, through these direct contacts or referrals through other people, to discover who, inside the company, may be in a position to hire you or refer you to someone who might.

In taking these first steps, it is important to remember how Mark got off track in our previous example, and recognize that you are in this for the long haul. You have not undertaken this process just to find a new employer or change some detail in your life. By successfully completing the A.I.M. process, you have put yourself on the path to become a much more resilient person than you are now. If unhappiness creeps up on you in the future or a change is thrust upon you by being fired or your relationship breaks up or some similar life-altering challenge occurs—you should be much better prepared both to anticipate that change and to respond to it using the principles of A.I.M. Specifically, your network should be part of your resilient response to any different or unfortunate situation. This network, coupled with an outlook informed by your increased self-knowledge gained through the early stages of the A.I.M. process, will be an asset that can get you through the difficult times we all experience.

From the initial meetings you have identified, map out other connections you can make to explore your options. Keep in mind what you have learned through the windowpane, decade in review, and the series of exercises that followed from the future options list. As your contacts provide feedback, think about what it may mean in the context of the options you have mapped out.

As you work through this initial list of potential contacts, you will probably notice obvious gaps. Most people, when starting this portion of A.I.M., quickly recognize that the people they know as part of their daily lives offer a good place to start strategic networking, but are often not the type of people who can support a thorough investigation of their options. In fact, I would submit that if you already have a diverse network of people you can consult about career and life changes, you are already well on the way to realizing A.I.M.'s ultimate goal of becoming more resilient through self-knowledge and a diverse support network.

When we conducted our research to construct a networking list, we included people with whom you had no personal connection, but wanted to make one. We also included, in our toolkit, an approach you could use for such people to increase your chances that they would take a meeting with you, but we also cautioned that such meetings are often very difficult to arrange. There are other ways than the dreaded cold call to meet people who are not in your immediate circle but who may be able to help you explore the options you have identified.

This is where we will spend most of our attention for this phase—working on the diverse ways you can find new contacts outside of your initial network.

Stage two: Finding new contacts and building networking into your daily life

The initial networking contacts you identified in your research and pursued in the first stage are just a start. While they may lead to success or to you attaining one of your initial goals, your chances of success increase greatly if you can leverage the work you have already done and meet as many people as possible who are relevant to your areas of interest. You can do this by seeking out new contacts and integrating regular networking activities into your daily life.

Where can you find these new contacts outside of the methods you have already identified? There are dozens of ways to meet new people in a professional manner and to find ways to learn from them. Most of these involve some strategic thinking on your part, to discover where the types of people you want to meet might congregate. Your best bet is to find existing networks and tap into them. No one assembles a network from a phone book, but countless others have met people through pre-existing networks and benefited greatly from it.

Keep in mind our earlier caution—make sure that you use your limited amount of time to deliver the best impact. While new experiences can lead to new networks, you may want to focus on the networks that you believe can help you attain your initial goals with A.I.M., phasing in broader networking activities as you move beyond them. The following are only a few general ideas for you to build upon while you search for the networks that will help you with your specific areas of interest, and to build broader-ranging networks that you can tap into in the long-term:

- **Community organizations:** Every community, whether it is a small town or large city, has a ready-made set of networks in its non-profit organizations and charities. These organizations are almost all mission-specific—there are different organizations for specific causes and issues—and each of these causes and issues will attract a certain network. If you are interested in a career with environmental aspects, for example, then you might look for an environmental, non-governmental organization that caters to the issues which interest you.

  By joining the organization, you will be put on their mailing list, be invited to member-only events and fundraisers, and have other opportunities that can bring you into contact with an entirely new network. Does health care interest you as a possible future option? You can always donate to a local hospital foundation and attend their fundraisers, or volunteer at a local hospice or health charity just to get some exposure in the field and begin to make contacts within it.

  These organizations also need boards of directors and, quite possibly, have other volunteer positions that might interest you. Boards are an excellent way to meet like-minded individuals who can see how well you operate in a strategic environment. Many community organizations also host events, fundraisers, and other gatherings that bring communities of interest together, both in person and on-line, to meet and discuss issues. These experiences, in addition to being uplifting, can also connect you with an entirely new range of people who would know a great deal about your area of interest.

- **Networking organizations:** Many communities have groups that come together specifically to promote networking. Chambers of commerce or boards of trade regularly meet to hear from speakers and encourage their members to meet others—and many such events have non-member rates. Other organizations such as Business Network International (BNI) or similar bodies bring people together for breakfast once a week to create business opportunities, so it is relatively easy to approach such organizations and ask to be a guest at one of their functions. Other groups organize regular "drink nights," luncheons, or after-work receptions, where people with a common interest can meet each other. My city, for example, hosts a regular gathering called "green drinks," where environmental activists, businesspeople, and those interested in the green issue get together once a month at a local pub to discuss issues and—you guessed it—network.

- **Professional organizations:** If you are a member of a profession, one option you might consider is to either join your professional association or, if you are already a member, become more active in it. Many associations offer networking events, meetings of local chapters, and the opportunity to serve on committees or boards of directors. This allows you to meet with people who share the same professional background, but may work in very different areas than your own.

- **Sports or activity leagues:** If you enjoy sports, leagues offer a great opportunity to meet people from a wide range of backgrounds, while helping you stay physically fit at the same time. This does not mean you have to join a masters basketball league or a similarly trying physical activity that may be beyond your ability. It could be as simple as joining a recreational league where people come together to play a game or two every week, and then go for a beer afterwards. There are also opportunities that can work for you even if you are injured. A former colleague of mine, after seriously injuring his back, joined a trivia league where people get together in a bar once a week to compete against one another. Aside from being a stress reliever, such activities offer you the chance to meet people from varying walks of life and, perhaps, make one or two connections that are transferable to your areas of interest.

- **University alumni associations:** If you attended college or university, most institutions have organizations that encourage their alumni to keep in touch. This could include regular receptions, events, volunteer committees, etc. The great thing about alumni groups is that they often contain people who work in quite diverse workplaces and who are plugged into various networks.

- **Speaker series:** Most communities of any size have regular speaker series run by different types of organizations. In my community alone, within the span of a week, I can attend luncheons by several distinct organizations such as the board of trade or different social clubs that offer receptions with speakers. These events offer great opportunities to meet others who have similar interests.

- **Houses of worship:** If you regularly attend a house of worship, such institutions offer excellent opportunities to meet others in your neighborhood while, at the same time, giving back to your community. Such local institutions, for example, often run programs for the homeless, have auxiliary clubs for men and women to raise money for various causes, and run evening groups that specifically help youth, disadvantaged families, or the poor in developing nations. There are excellent opportunities to meet— and help—others through a house of worship.

- **Political parties:** Major political parties, if you are so inclined, are often excellent places to meet engaged people with values and beliefs similar to your own. They offer opportunities on a number of levels, by volunteering on local committees, helping local candidates, participating in on-line discussions, attending fundraising receptions, or attending local or national conventions. While your political affiliation may not be something you want to advertise when you are networking broadly, if you are politically minded and want to meet people, they do offer excellent opportunities.

A word about on-line communities

You will note that we have not spent a great deal of time discussing on-line opportunities to meet others and discuss your options and build your future networks. While on-line social media offer great ways to learn about specific areas and connect with different communities, they are generally not useful for building the trust that is needed to make networking a true asset for you.

Facebook is a good example. The on-line social networking site boasts more than 300 million members and millions of groups that its members can join to discuss different issues. It is very easy to join these groups and become "friends" with those you meet through them. You can even share an on-line discussion or an e-mail with your new on-line network, yet would you be likely to give a phone number or other personal information about a contact to someone you had only met on-line? I didn't think so.

Other than for research purposes, different sites and mailing lists are particularly useful when they plug you in to local events that you may not have been aware of otherwise. Almost every organization of a certain size publishes an on-line newsletter that, in addition to sharing information, often lists volunteer opportunities and upcoming events that the organization might be holding. Getting on these mailing lists connects you to a steady flow of information about a new community you may want to learn more about, so this is an option you should definitely consider.

Practical advice on getting the most out of networking

The following are some tips and tricks you should keep in mind as you explore your options and move to make networking part of your regular work and personal life:

Get the numbers to work for you

As you move out into the world and begin meeting with people beyond your initial contact list, it is easy to get discouraged if things don't immediately go your way. You might call or e-mail a few people or approach someone at an event and get the brush off.

Don't sweat it. Volume matters. If you ask enough people, you will get through to new and interesting people who can help you in ways you might not have even thought possible. My co-writer, Alex, has a great story about a friend of his, Johann, and how he met his wife. Johann is now in his late thirties, a happily married telecommunications executive with a small child. When he was single, however, he was a big proponent of what he called the "volume theory" of dating. After seeing a number of women, none seriously, through his twenties, he decided at the age of thirty-two that it was time to get serious. He wanted to find a suitable life partner, one with whom he shared core values.

Johann's approach should be familiar to those who have adopted the A.I.M. method. He began by thinking long and hard about what he wanted out of a relationship and what he could offer to a prospective spouse. He also looked at promising relationships from his past which had not worked out, and asked himself, "Why?" He also asked the advice of close friends. Armed with a better knowledge of the mistakes he may have made in the past—and what he wanted in a future partner—he then began to change his routine to increase the chances he would meet someone with whom he might fall in love and start a family.

Aside from posting profiles on popular Internet dating sites, he also asked his friends, including Alex, if they knew anyone to whom they could introduce him. Never a fan of singles bars, he also ramped up the number of other social events he attended that might be frequented by new and interesting people in his age range. Each week, he found new ways to meet dozens of new people in a variety of settings. As his social network grew, so too did the number of people who either asked him on a date or rejected him when he began to explore that option. He also, surprisingly, met a large number of people who, when they learned he was single, said, "I have this friend who would be great for you!" Within a few months, he was dating regularly again, much to the amusement of Alex and his other friends.

"I know falling in love isn't a formula," he said, responding to some good-natured teasing, "but you've got to meet a lot of people and get turned down a lot before you date some of them, and then you have to date a lot more to find someone that you develop that special bond with. But in the end, it will be worth it."

Within a year of expanding his networks and maximizing his opportunities to meet others, Johann was dating someone seriously.

Within two years, they were married and now have a young child with another on the way.

Alex contrasts Johann's story with that of another friend. Kevin is a graphic designer with an interesting job and he has a lot of likable personal qualities. Kevin's philosophy towards meeting a life partner can best be summed up as, "If it's meant to happen, it will happen." Kevin works long hours and, exhausted most evenings, makes his way home to watch a bit of TV before returning to work the next day. He rarely varies this routine, keeping in touch with the same friends and following the same schedule. While Kevin is an attractive person, he currently dates infrequently and, while he confessed to Alex that he would like to get married, he does not have any serious prospects on the horizon.

These two examples clearly illustrate the power of a good network, of not taking negative feedback too seriously, and of a positive, open attitude. Kevin played it safe—and is still waiting for a change to happen. Johann was strategic, got out there, and did something about it—and is now moving in the direction he wants.

Go where the "cool things" are happening

People tend to gather in like-minded groups. Political parties attract people with certain ideas about how the world works. Arts groups attract those who value creativity and expression. Business groups attract those who value the bottom line. For the purposes of your networking, the types of dynamic, well-connected people who can link you with others tend to gather with those who have a similar orientation or outlook.

One of my former clients once received some interesting advice in this respect when he was beginning the networking phase of A.I.M. A professional in his early thirties who was just starting to think strategically about his career, Andre was in the initial stages of moving from a well-paying position that he found "incredibly boring" to finding something else that would challenge his creative side. One of the networking contacts he made through a friend was a CEO who had a history of working in dynamic organizations. When Andre met with him, he only offered one piece of advice.

"Son," he told Andre, "just go where the neat stuff is happening."

He went on to explain that, in his experience, there are always interesting things happening in society that attract interesting people. There are segments of our society and economy where things don't change that much from year to year (such as most professions, large parts of education and government, large multinational companies, etc.) and then there are other parts where interesting people come together to discuss issues and try to find solutions.

At the time Andre was meeting the CEO, for example, the city in which they both lived was trying to figure out how to redevelop its waterfront. The issues were dominating the local news coverage day after day, with citizens' groups, governments, zoning agencies, and new industries all trying to figure out what to do.

"If I were you," the CEO told Andre, "I'd find issues like that, issues that are attracting a lot of attention, and find ways to meet with the people who are trying to solve them. I can guarantee that you will meet a lot of smart, interesting people who will open your eyes to new issues and to new networks."

Andre took his advice and, armed with a few referrals from the CEO, met with several of the key people who were working on the waterfront issue. Within a few months, he found himself working in a senior position at a local nonprofit agency that was coordinating community input on the waterfront redesign. While this position fit well with the values and options he had identified through the A.I.M. process, the actual job would never have occurred to him had he not opened his network to new and interesting options.

Find the connector in the crowd

When you begin building regular networking efforts into your regular personal and professional life, you will begin to spot different types of people who are common to every crowd. Every event, for example, will have its share of wallflowers who don't feel comfortable starting conversations. There will be the extreme extroverts, in one form or another, who want to be the center of attention. And there will be the people that social commentator Malcolm Gladwell calls "connectors." These are the people you want to get to know.

By their simple definition, connectors are simply those "who know a lot of other people." In any society, most of us know a good number of friends and acquaintances, but there are a small number of us who know many times the number of people that is considered a normal social network. For whatever reason, sprinkled throughout society are people who are at the center of overlapping networks, and when asked, they can connect you with a lot of other people.

One of my first coaching clients, Eric, was lucky enough to strike just such a connector very early in his initial networking. Eric was a young public relations professional who wanted to explore whether he should shift from the world of in-house PR to working for an agency. While he was happy being the youngest director of communications in the history of his organization, he wanted to explore his options.

With coaching, he identified a number of senior people at different agencies and began to ask people in his network if they could introduce him to one of them. As luck would have it, a good friend did know one of them and furnished Eric with an introduction. In a 15-minute information interview, after hearing Eric's elevator speech and assessing what he was looking to do, the connector pulled out his BlackBerry and promptly said, "Here are some people you have to meet." He then proceeded to provide Eric with the names and contact information for more than twenty senior people at a variety of organizations, from ad agencies to educational institutions to senior people in government.

Eric was pleased at our next meeting at how the meeting had gone but, humorously, didn't realize how lucky he had been to hit a connector on his second meeting.

"I think it went well, Jim," he said. "He offered to connect me with a few interesting people."

When I reviewed the names the CEO had suggested, it read like a who's who of the influencers who made several different industries work. Eric was able to use the name of his connector to open doors at offices all over the city. And while he eventually ruled out a shift into the agency world, he did uncover several other opportunities that opened up new and exciting possibilities for him.

Don't worry: Confidence can be learned

Armies all over the world have figured out something unique. They can, in the relatively short amount of time that a recruit spends at boot camp, get people to act completely contrary to their instincts. One of their biggest achievements, for example, is to teach people that, when they are being shot at, they should face in the direction of the gunfire and do something about it. This is completely against human instinct. Your natural reaction—and that of anyone who has not been through military training—would be to run as quickly as they can in the opposite direction or find a place to hide until the shooting stops. But militaries have found that, with the right kind of attitude and training, you can help people overcome a gut instinct and do something quite different.

I always think about that example when some of my coaching clients express discomfort and self-doubt about having to talk to people they don't know in a social situation. While we have gone a long way towards taking the uncertainty out of a formal networking meeting with the scripts we reviewed in our toolkit chapter, many of my clients are still uncertain about unscripted situations. "What if I have to go to a cocktail reception or a luncheon?" they ask. "What in heaven's name will I say to people I don't know?"

This is a common concern for many people. We are taught, largely, to be a little reserved around people we don't know. But there is good news. As the boot camp example shows, confidence in strange situations can be learned.

Imagine you are attending a reception where the types of people you would like to add to your network are gathering. A simple series of steps can help you confront your fear and overcome it. Start when you are entering the room. Ask the person at the door how they are doing and follow up with a few questions, such as, "How many people are you expecting to attend tonight?" or "This looks like a popular event, how does it compare to the last one you held?"

Continue the offensive once you move into the crowd. Remember that everyone feels a little awkward in crowds, so think of it as your job to help others feel a little more comfortable by giving them an opportunity to talk. Don't be shy—use a few simple opening questions such as, "Hi, what brings you here today?" or "I'm just ran-domly introducing myself to people. Hi, I'm _____." Usually that is all it takes to start one conversation that can then lead to others. Once you have begun speaking to a few people and others walk into range, try to include them in the conversation. When you see people walking by on their own, stop them and say, "Hi, can I introduce you to _____ (the person you just met)?" This forces them to introduce themselves, and then allows you to ask a few questions that will lead to a deeper conversation. With these simple techniques, what some of my clients would see as a painful challenge—working a room to meet some new people—suddenly becomes a productive evening where you may meet several people with whom you can follow up with a phone call or e-mail the next day.

Focus on trust, and networking will follow

Any networking process is built on context and on trust. Both of these qualities are essential to successful networking. Context comes from your story, the process we began at the start of A.I.M. It allows you to answer the basic question that any networking contact might have: "Who are you and why are you meeting with me?"

Trust is another important component, as any referrals net-working contacts will provide to you will be based, in large part, on whether they trust you to be a good representative in their judgment. If a contact says, "I think you should meet my colleague John," they are essentially saying to their colleague, "I have made a judgment that, by recommending you meet with this person, they are worth meeting. They won't waste your time and, if you take the time to meet with them, you may be able to help them."

If this does not turn out to be true, John will certainly let your contact know and their relationship may suffer. Therefore, focus on building trust into your networking relationships and they will strengthen and grow as a result. Be on time. Be honest with your contacts. If you commit to follow up, be sure to do so. If they call you to ask a favor of you, help them gladly without any thought of recompense. These and other behaviors reinforce trust. And trust makes networking work.

When it all comes together: Henry's networking challenges and successes

A few chapters ago, we met Henry. He was the young engineering executive who, facing some issues with his current employer, undertook the A.I.M. process to identify some potential options and directions in which he could take his career. From a feeling of uncertainty and a few initial ideas that looked very promising, Henry had explored his values and motivations and identified four distinct options that he wanted to explore:

HENRY'S FUTURE OPTIONS LIST	Staying where I am?	Another big company?	Smaller, entrepreneurial company?	Join a consulting practice?
	Stick it out and take my chances, since I have been treated well, there is no reason to think my successful career path should not continue.	The head-hunters tell me I am in demand, so maybe there is another big company out there that might give me more freedom.	I am intrigued about this possibility as I have seen friends who have made this kind of move, and they seem to feel fulfilled and their ideas are being appreciated.	With my experience in operations and planning, is this the time to go into consulting and enhance my skills even more, probably with a large consulting shop that houses "best practices in my field?"
Ideal role	Current position	Similar to current position	Unknown	Unknown
Passion	Some.	Some.	Definitely.	Some.
Good at it	Yes.	Yes, if the job is similar.	Think I can do it.	I think my experience is transferable.
Windowpane fit	Yes; status quo and safe.	Some red flags, as it might disrupt things.	Could be high risk financially and personal strain.	Travel may be at odds with my family values.
Cost	No immediate cost to me.	Don't know my market value yet—it may be lower than where I am now.	If I have to put my own money into the firm, we can't afford that right now.	Unknown but varying income levels of some consultants could upset our financial plans.
Time	None, as I have already committed the time.	I could explore this one with a few meetings.	This would take a big time commitment to explore, as I don't know this world.	A few meetings with the bigger firms should tell me if I am interested in this one.

When we left Henry's story a few chapters ago, he had asked himself some "hard questions" about his options. He had also begun some baby steps into the networking world by meeting with a few former business acquaintances to get their ideas on who he might meet to gather more research on his options. Finally, he had "cashed a reality check" with his close friend and former colleague Matt, who had once worked at Henry's firm. Matt's contribution was invaluable. He queried the impact that some of Henry's options might have on his family, and he also raised some questions about whether Henry was really suited to making the jump into a more entrepreneurial firm at this point in his life. Matt had also confirmed for Henry that his suspicion that his current employer might be a takeover target was correct.

This feedback left Henry in a good position to begin some more formal networking activities. Matt had essentially helped Henry rule out, for now, making an immediate leap from his current employer into a more entrepreneurial organization. Henry opted to forgo the immediate possibility of a new position at another firm to stay at his current company and explore his options there, while also continuing to build his network outside his current firm and see what options that might uncover. Matt's validation of Henry's takeover concerns also gave Henry his first networking target—the CEO of his current firm.

While Henry was on a first-name basis with the CEO, they were not close colleagues. Henry's suspicion that the firm might be taken over was not common knowledge within the firm, so any approach on that front had to be taken carefully. Building on the work he had done to fill up his toolkit, Henry crafted a strategic approach to his CEO, asking for a meeting to discuss "some strategic issues with the company and how we might move forward with them." The CEO agreed to take the meeting, and Henry spent more than an hour talking with him about his observations on the strategic issues with the company, how he saw it positioned in the marketplace, and, more delicately, what role Henry might play as the firm moved forward to deal with these issues.

Henry reported to me that the CEO was interested in his opinions, but had hedged his bets about whether the firm might be taken over.

"Henry," he had said, "even if the company was in play, I couldn't share that information with you. Let me just say that your observations about this firm and where it can improve are bang on. I think there will be good opportunities for you as we move ahead, so I look forward to talking with you more about it soon."

Henry was encouraged and a little puzzled at the same time. By not vehemently denying that a takeover was a possibility, the CEO had essentially told Henry that it might be in the cards. He had also taken the time to reinforce that he appreciated Henry's strategic thinking about the future of the firm and saw a role for him in that future. Altogether, this was a positive outcome for Henry's first formal networking meeting.

Confident that things on the "home front" with his current job were fairly secure, Henry next turned his networking attention to exploring some of his other options. He had determined through the "hard questions" and "reality check" phases of A.I.M. that his ideas of working in a consulting role or for another company similar in size to his current employer were his two most promising options. While Henry found the idea of working for a smaller, more entrepreneurial company very interesting, he had serious concerns that this option might involve significantly more risks than he was willing to take, given his status as the sole breadwinner for his family and the young age of his children. He would explore this option, but as a third priority behind looking at another company and learning more about consulting.

His first step as he looked to network outside his current firm was to meet with his friend Matt again. Without betraying any company secrets, he took Matt for coffee and briefed him on the basic outcome of his meeting with the CEO. They discussed his plans to prioritize the other two options and, at the end of the meeting, Henry asked if Matt would connect him with others in his industry who could help him learn more about firms of a similar size. He also asked about

Matt's earlier offer to formally connect him with the consulting contact that he had mentioned in their first meeting. Matt quickly agreed. He trusted that Henry would represent himself well in any meetings he might arrange, so he offered to connect him with two people who worked in senior roles in competing companies, and with a former colleague of his who was now a senior partner in a consulting firm.

Following the principles of A.I.M., Henry had started with "easy" networking meetings by approaching people he knew to get the ball rolling. Back in his office after their meeting, Henry quickly sent Matt a "thank you" e-mail for offering the three new contacts. He then began conducting a bit of additional research on the three people Matt had recommended: Lynn and Chen were both senior managers at two of Henry's competing firms, while Oscar was the consulting partner. Henry spent that evening surfing the Internet to learn more about each of these contacts, looking at their profiles on business social media sites such as LinkedIn and reading the annual reports that he downloaded from the Internet. The next day, he called all three, using a variant of the networking script he had developed as part of his toolkit. It went something like this:

> "Hi, Lynn. My name is Henry Rousseau. Matt Davies suggested I call you. I've known Matt for ten years, when we used to work together at XYZ Company. I still work there but am currently conducting a few interviews to see how others are doing in the industry and what my longer-term options are. I'm wondering if you have time to have a coffee and chat. Would next Wednesday afternoon or the following Tuesday morning work for you?"

As luck would have it, he was able to talk to two of the contacts in person and quickly confirmed two meetings for the following week. He was unable to get in touch with the third contact, but followed up with an e-mail and another call and was able to book a meeting in two weeks' time.

Henry was a little worried, but encouraged. He met with me prior to doing these meetings. "Jim, this is a big step. I don't know these people and I feel like I am being disloyal to my current company. My CEO seems to want me to stick around, and here I am meeting with two of his competitors and a company that might, conceivably, offer me a consulting position. What should I do?"

This is a common question from many of my clients. Most of us are not encouraged to be selfish—for good reason. No one likes a person who is obviously in it for him or herself. Yet, too little selfishness is often a problem. Every year, thousands of people are laid off from companies to which they were quite loyal. Had they spent a bit more time looking at their options and developing an external network, they might have been better able to weather the surprise layoff. This does not mean you do not commit 100 percent to your current employer—that is your job and it's always the right thing to do. But what it does mean is that you treat your current job as just that—your current job. As such, it is only one chapter of an ongoing story of your life and career, so you should always be thinking about how to prepare yourself for the changes that may be coming.

"Well, Henry," I cautioned him, "you are not selling secrets to these firms, but merely establishing contacts and trying to learn more about your options. There is nothing disloyal in that, and the people you are meeting should understand this."

Encouraged, he went ahead and held meetings with all three, providing them with his one-page profile in advance, to save time and share the purpose of the meeting. From those meetings, Henry learned some interesting things.

He met with Oscar the consultant in a coffee shop close to his office. Oscar was a pleasant man in his early fifties who began by thanking him for the one-page profile and, after hearing a little more about Henry and his challenge, said those four magic words that are golden when networking: "How can I help?"

Over the next hour, their conversation covered a lot of ground. Henry talked about his current situation, reinforcing that while he was happy, he was broadening his horizons by doing some networking around several options that interested him, including consulting. He had hired several consultants in his role as director of manufacturing, and suspected that some experience in the field might stand him in good stead if he wanted to move on to become a general manager or CEO.

Oscar shared his own career path and background. He had begun work as an engineer working at the processing plants for a mining company before making a shift in his early thirties to the consulting world, where he had worked ever since. They spoke in great detail about the skill base required to thrive in the consulting world, with Oscar stressing the need to be good at analysis and problem solving, to have some technical expertise in a particular field, to have the ability to lead a project team and get things done. Then he talked about the need to mentally shift from the employee mindset—of doing the work—to the advisory mindset of thinking strategically about how the work might be done better.

"If I were to transition into a consulting position," Henry asked, "what do you think the biggest change I would face in the first few years would be?"

Oscar paused, and then began, "I think there are two things, Henry. First, you have great industry experience so a consulting firm would be interested in what you have to offer. Secondly, the amount of travel in the first few years could be a little stressful. I'd estimate that as much as 50 percent of your work in those first years could be on the road as you build up your skill set and client base."

That gave Henry pause to think. His windowpane had stressed the importance of spending time with his young family, so this was definitely something to consider. In closing, Henry thanked Oscar and asked if there were other people he would recommend he speak with about his search. Oscar promptly recommended that he speak with two colleagues of his who worked at different manufacturing firms, as well as someone who ran a smaller consultancy than Oscar's.

"It might do you some good to talk with people at different-sized firms," Oscar offered, "as they might have a different perspective from the one I could give you."

As they were leaving the coffee shop, Oscar wanted to share one more thing with Henry. "I do a lot of these networking meetings," Oscar said, "and rarely do I see someone so well prepared. The one-page profile was impressive. I'd love to talk with you once you've had your meetings to learn more about this process."

Henry thanked him again and committed to follow up in a few weeks with more information on the A.I.M. process.

Henry's meetings with his two contacts, Chen and Lynn, who worked at comparable manufacturing firms yielded similarly positive results. Both were happy to meet with him and readily shared their knowledge about their industries in general, and their firms in particular. As had been the case with Oscar, they readily offered several suggestions about others that Henry should meet with as he explored his options. From his meetings with the three contacts, Henry now had more than ten additional people that he could call. As you can see, a domino effect was starting to take hold, where initial contacts led to several more that he could then trust to lead to still more meetings. From his initial foray into the networking world, Henry had now booked dozens of meetings that would take him a few months to work through. When he met with me a few weeks after starting his networking phase, it was clear that the beginning of an extended network for Henry was taking shape.

"Jim," he shared enthusiastically, "I have to admit I didn't think it would happen this quickly, but all the work we put into preparation seems to be paying off."

I told him he should be proud of the work he had done, but I cautioned him that—like Mark—he should not declare victory too early. He had ruled out the consulting option for now, judging that it would take him away from his young family for too much time. But he still had one option that he had not yet really explored—working for an entrepreneurial company. He had been very enthusiastic about the idea, but also knew that it might pose too much risk to his financial security, at least at this stage of his life. The only way he would know for sure was to get out and meet people in the field.

"Your interviews are booked well into the next two months for your other option," I advised. "You might want to see if you can do a few quick meetings to explore your investment option, if only to rule it out so you can focus entirely on the ones you have left."

Henry agreed. Before looking for networking contacts, however, he went back to the original research that he had conducted. Heeding the caution he had received from Matt earlier in the process when he had questioned whether Henry knew what it meant to be an entrepreneur, he visited a bookstore and came away with several biographies of entrepreneurs and reference books on the topic.

From this research, he realized that two common characteristics of entrepreneurs are: 1) they have a strong ability to tolerate risk; and 2) they have generally reached a point in their lives when they are tired of working for other people. With this in mind, Henry revisited his windowpane exercise to see what it might tell him about his own predispositions in these areas.

Professional	*Personal*
• I have spent fifteen successful years in a multinational company.	• I am happily married with two kids in primary school.
• I have strong operations and planning skills.	• We own our own home (with a $150,000 mortgage).
• I want to be a general manager in a company in this field.	• I am the sole wage earner with a low six-figure package.
• I wonder whether I would do better in a smaller, entrepreneurial company.	• We like the town in which we live. We have lots of friends and are very active in the community.
• My company may be sold and that may throw a wrench into my career.	• I am generally not a risk taker.
• Headhunters say I am very marketable.	

Physical	Spiritual
• I work out regularly, eat well, and generally maintain good health.	• I am very loyal to my company and my staff.
• I play hockey once a week with the guys.	• I am a team player and seek lots of input from my staff.
• We ski and do other outdoor sports as a family.	• Giving back to my community through my church and charities is important to me.
	• I am very trusting and trustworthy.
	• Work-life balance is vital to me.

Given what this exercise told him about himself, Henry began to suspect that a role focused entirely on entrepreneurship may not be a good fit for him. He valued "loyalty" to a company, and placed a premium on "work-life balance." He was a "team player" who valued "input" from those with whom he worked. He was the sole bread-winner and liked living in the community where they had chosen to raise their family. Most importantly, he had described himself as "not a risk taker." Setting up his own firm from scratch or joining a small firm with big plans would pose a considerable challenge to these values.

From his future options list, however, he had noted that he was most passionate about the idea of working for a firm with entrepreneurial tendencies. In a subsequent conversation with me, he asked an interesting question: "Jim, do you think I could find a dynamic, smaller company—one that works with entrepreneurs or has a very creative workplace—that might not be so at odds with my core values?"

Henry was now thinking two or three steps ahead, which at this stage of the process is good to see. He was already trying to reconcile what he had learned in the earlier stages of A.I.M. with what he was continuing to learn about himself. I encouraged him to explore this option further, so he engaged a few people in his emerging network to ask them the same question. After a few e-mails, phone calls, and one very solid introduction from a close friend of Lynn's, he found himself sitting in the office of a small investment firm that provided venture capital to start-up enterprises.

Joel, the CEO of the firm, was intrigued by Henry and his journey, and readily explained how his firm operated. He noted that they were very entrepreneurial and were comprised of three partners, with each holding an equal number of shares. Joel had spent decades in large investment firms before moving out on his own with his two partners. Together, they had built a well-regarded boutique firm that catered to small manufacturing start-ups. It was clear from Joel's description that he loved his job and took tremendous pride in how they had built their firm from nothing. It was also clear that the firm was doing well financially. It would probably be able to pay Henry very well, provided they were interested and thought there might be a fit.

This led Henry to ask a key question: "Joel, suppose you were me? You're in your late thirties with a young family. You're doing okay in the manufacturing business, but might want to explore working for a firm like this. What would you do?"

This type of question is a good one. It doesn't ask the person on the other side of the desk for a job. It asks him or her to give you advice, based on what they know about you—and about firms like the one they work in.

Joel considered Henry's question for just a moment before giving him a clear answer.

"I would put a few more years in to broaden your experience, Henry," he said. "You've got solid credentials when it comes to manufacturing, but a firm like ours would require quite a learning curve on the financial side. If you had worked in a firm that had been through a major financing or a takeover that would really help."

Henry smiled when he told me this story a few days later. He had been able to rule out this kind of position right away, but it opened up an interesting option not too far down the road.

"Jim," he said, chuckling, "I just might have the opportunity to learn a lot about mergers and acquisitions at my current job in the next few months."

Henry's story shows the value of taking the early stages of the A.I.M. process seriously, and spending an appropriate amount of time on all of the elements. Henry was able to hit the ground running and quickly build what would become a very solid network because he was well prepared. His contacts noted how focused his efforts were, and he was able to quickly learn from what he heard, revisit his earlier exercises, and use them to respond and move forward. Contrast this with Mark's experience, where he had jumped too soon and his lead quickly ran out. It was only by reconnecting with the process that he was able to put in the time that was necessary to make the best use of his networking opportunities.

Moving forward to "A.I.M. in constant motion"

With these techniques and the accompanying stories that demonstrate how A.I.M. can deliver results in its final networking stages, it would seem that our journey is at an end. If Henry has determined what his best course of action is, made a decision to stay, and is also busy building a better network—isn't that it? Hasn't he accomplished what he set out to do?

Yes and no. While he now has a new perspective on the challenges he faces—and a powerful new asset in his growing network—there is still one phase of A.I.M. that both you and Henry have to work through. That is when the principles behind the A.I.M. method become part of your normal work and personal life, and you are in a position not to just focus on your challenges, but you can start to assist other people through your example and your skills. This is the focus of our final A.I.M. stage: "A.I.M. in Constant Motion."

CHAPTER 12

A.I.M. in Constant Motion

The habit of giving only enhances the desire to give.

—Walt Whitman

With this chapter, our journey through the ten steps of the A.I.M. process nears its end. Over the previous nine stages, we have identified your main challenge and, through several exercises, explored what you value and how that can impact what you are seeking to change. Your windowpane and decade review exercises helped you capture values and past patterns, while your future options list allowed you to brainstorm about areas you might want to investigate. Giving you the ability to reflect which these exercises provided, coupled with the perspective offered by a few outside sources, helped you focus and prioritize your options. You could then lay the groundwork through research and explore them further through a focused networking strategy. As we shared these steps, we also met dozens of people who have faced the same types of challenges that you have faced, and who overcame them by applying a method used by executives from around the world.

At this point in the process you may be feeling comfortable. If you have followed the method correctly, you should be well on the way to addressing the concern you identified in your focus statement in one of the early stages of the A.I.M. process. Perhaps your networking efforts have already begun to reveal a path forward—a new job, a new start, or a new direction. It would be normal to think, after the ninth stage of A.I.M., that your task is complete. Haven't you addressed what you set out to do? Haven't you begun to build a network that will not only help you address your focus statement, but also will help you become more resilient and in charge of your life as you move forward? Yes, you may have, but the A.I.M. process does not reach its ultimate stage until you complete one final piece of your evolution.

The first nine stages of A.I.M. were all about the first letter of A.I.M.: "achieve." These stages were about your challenges and your needs. The techniques outlined in these chapters showed you how to identify and address your issues so that you could achieve an appropriate solution. The final stage of A.I.M. deals with the other two letters of A.I.M., those representing "inspire" and "make a difference." Specifically, this final stage focuses on how, as you continue to grow and use the A.I.M. process, you can begin to give back to others, just as the A.I.M. process has given to you.

Why give back?

While few people would be as blunt at this stage as to ask: "Why bother to give back?" it is a valid question. I have had a few clients ask me that very question, "Surely, Jim, we have done enough work through this process? I've addressed my problems—isn't that what the process was all about?"

Yes . . . and no. This process was about changing something that made you unhappy. To see A.I.M. through to its successful conclusion, you need to ingrain A.I.M.'s principles into your everyday life to ensure that you continue to move forward and do not return to your previous state. In many ways, it is similar to the process undertaken by people who are dissatisfied with their physical fitness or appearance. They invest considerable time in going to the gym or rigidly following a diet, only to slide back to where they started once they attain their initial goals, abandoning the changes they have made in their lifestyle. People who are serious about their wellness will tell you that fitness is not about one diet, going to the gym for a few months, or running a few laps. Becoming truly fit is about a comprehensive approach to life that puts wellness first, and informs the way in which you approach living. Fit people eat well, making dietary choices at every meal that reinforce their lifestyle. People who are fit look for opportunities to build physical activity into their daily lives, taking the stairs instead of an elevator or escalator, taking a break to walk at lunch or getting off the bus a few stops early and walking home. They take their running shoes or workout gear on vacation or business trips, squeezing in a workout at the and of the day in a hotel weight room, or an early-morning run before their meetings. Fit people, in short, find ways to maintain their hard-won advantage by making fitness an unquestioned part of their everyday life, to the point that the choices they make to reinforce their gains are largely unconscious. It simply becomes part of what they do.

Such is the case with A.I.M. By integrating A.I.M. principles into your everyday life, it becomes part of who you are and how you approach your life. Networking, for example, is not something that you do just to address the challenge you outlined in your focus statement. Building and engaging your network becomes something you do every week, at every gathering, through every business and personal encounter. Without realizing it, you will be building one of the most valuable assets a person can have—a supportive network of people whom you can call upon to help you in challenging times.

The single greatest A.I.M. principle you can integrate into your life as you near the end of the process is the open, helpful orientation that should underlie all good networking. Just as others were open to your calls and meetings when you began networking, it is now your turn to be open to helping others. When you do this, your motivation should be simply to help others who approach you. Now, when someone approaches you, either by a cold call or a referral, you only have to say five words: "How can I help you?" You should not be thinking, "How can this person help me?" or "Hmmm . . . maybe not, this could be a waste of time."

Even those clients who have followed the process diligently and produced significant positive momentum by the ninth stage become uneasy when we discuss the tenth and final stage. It is a challenge for some people to shift from what has largely been a self-centered process to one that asks them to now look outward and help others. At the root is a simple question: "What's in this for me?"

Let us put aside for a moment the fact that you have, most likely, been able to attain positive results with the A.I.M. process through the generosity of other people. Throughout the process you have relied on help from others. Alex and I have outlined the method and shared it with you through this book. At several points—including when you cashed your reality check and reached out to start your network—you relied on others to help you get going. Through the ups and downs you have faced, you have probably relied on friends, family, or a partner who has supported your search. When you began to network with a growing number of people, you depended on their generosity with their time, advice, and contacts. It makes perfect sense to emulate their example and begin to give back, but let's put that aside for a moment.

Let's also set aside the obvious moral arguments in favor of giving back. It would be fairly easy to argue that helping others "is just the right thing to do." Human beings have an ingrained desire to help others, and this desire is made all the more pressing when we begin to succeed. When we are successful, most of us are conscious that there are others who have not yet made it to this level, so we feel a motivation to give back, a motivation that comes from a deep, and moral, part of our being. Let us put this moral reason aside as well.

While these reasons should provide more than enough motivation to embrace A.I.M.'s call to give back, there is another very practical—and selfish—reason for you to help others. Helping others may, according to new research, make you happier and more economically successful.

Arthur C. Brooks is a U.S. social theorist, an academic at Syracuse University in upstate New York and the president of a Washington-based think tank. He has always been concerned with how society functions—specifically, which behaviors contribute to the success or failure of individuals and communities. In 2005, he conducted a study on the relationship between giving, volunteering, and happiness in his book *Who Really Cares*. Among the many questions Brooks addressed, was a basic one: Why do wealthy people give more money to charity?

His observation is an objective one, supported by census data that clearly shows that people who earn more money give the most to charity. At first glance this may seem self-evident. "Of course they do," one might say. "They have more money to give, therefore they can afford it." Brooks, however, proposed a unique theory. He hypothesized that having an orientation towards giving *causes* people to become wealthy and societies to become more success-ful. Individual giving, he suggests, is based upon a belief that one *should* give back. And holding such a belief leads a person to become economically successful.

Brooks goes on to cite data on average incomes to support this point. He notes that if you compare two people who are identical in education, age, religion, politics, sex, and race where one person regularly gives and volunteers and the other does not, the person with the giving orientation earns, on average, $14,000 more per year than their comparator. Moreover, he has found that if some-one begins to regularly give and volunteer, such behavior causes that person's income to rise in subsequent years. Put another way, the giving behavior in most cases *precedes* their economic suc-cess. It can, therefore, be argued that people do not give to char-ity because they have money, they have a giving orientation *first*, which allows them to *later* make enough money to increase their donations to charity. An orientation towards giving back, it would seem, has the selfish result of making the giver more successful down the road.

"When I give," Brooks writes, "I become happier, healthier, and more successful . . . I am by definition a provider of help, as opposed to a victim. When I am thus empowered, my life improves in all sorts of ways."[1] This outward mental orientation towards giving, Brooks suggests, makes people more resilient. They are able to escape from poverty more quickly and able to succeed with their families and in their workplaces in ways that more inward-looking comparators may not. By taking control of the way we choose to treat others, we can orient ourselves in a manner that will produce better individual and social outcomes.

Deep down, is this really a surprise to us? While some of Brooks's supporters use his findings to posit the involvement of a higher power in "rewarding" such giving behavior, there is a simpler explanation that I think we can all understand and appreciate. If you have a giving, outward-looking orientation that focuses on the good you can do not just for yourself but also for others, such an orientation probably makes you more likely to succeed at whatever you choose to do in life. It will allow you to appreciate opportunities and take advantage of them, rather than sulking in a fog of disengagement or blaming others for your problems. It will draw other people to you, people who may be able to help you in whatever area you choose to work. And while such an open orientation won't protect you from being blindsided by the occasional missteps that befall us all (such as unexpected changes at work, layoffs, or illness), its ingrained optimism should be able to help you bounce back quickly from a setback.

One of my long-term coaching clients, Brandon, is a good example of optimism in action. I coached Brandon over a five-year period, beginning when he was the young CEO of a database storage business. Dissatisfied with the long hours and constant pressure of a growing firm, he used the A.I.M. process to transition while he was at the top of his game. After examining his passions, his values, and his options, he started his own business offering IT consulting services to the financial services industry. By the end of our coaching relationship, he was enjoying the freedom of running his own show, splitting his time

---

[1] Arthur Brooks. *Who Really Cares.* New York: Basic Books, 2006 p. 142.

between his business, life at his new cottage, and spending more time sharing the responsibilities of raising his young family. Despite having achieved so much through the process, Brandon still felt something was missing. One day, as our engagement was ending, he confided that he really wanted to begin giving something back.

"Jim," he said, "I know I have been incredibly fortunate. I really want to make sure I get this last phase right and begin to help others in the best way I can."

In the following months, he became one of the most active people I know in the networking realm, meeting with dozens of people each month to offer his advice and counsel. Through his complete willingness to help others, he found that additional clients were contacting him out of the blue, having been referred to him by new contacts—even though he had not actively sought to use networking to expand his already prosperous business.

"Jim," he confided to me, "I didn't set out to grow my business by being generous, but that seems to be what happened!"

While Brandon's experience shows the personal rewards one can achieve by giving back, one only has to look at the example of Jean Vanier to see that the principles that underlie this final phase of A.I.M. do not just result in individual or career success. They can be put to a much higher use. Vanier was a son of privilege, born into one of the most illustrious families in Canada. His father, General Georges Vanier, served as governor general of the country. The younger Vanier, however, took a different path to public service. In 1964, moved by the suffering he saw in a psychiatric hospital in France that housed thousands of children with severe disabilities, he founded a nonprofit organization called by its French name, *L'arche*, or "the ark."

His initial vision was modest. He wanted people with profound disabilities to live in the community as equals, in a way that could enrich their lives and the lives of those they lived with. With little more than that in mind, and without a formal plan, he invited two people with severe disabilities to leave their institution and live with him. In the years that followed, something special began to happen.

Others were moved by Vanier's selfless example and wanted to help. In his encounters with the curious, he was open, sharing the story of what had brought him to this point. He freely shared his time and effort, talking to anyone who would listen about the difference we all might make if we became engaged and gave to causes and issues we cared about.

The results have been inspiring. From this initial beginning, L'arche now has 131 homes around the world that have built upon Vanier's initial idea that those with disabilities can live full lives with others in the community, with the benefit of both the able and disabled gaining from their partnership. Although now retired from his day-to-day duties at L'arche, Vanier writes and lectures widely on the ideas that led to the creation of this groundbreaking organization. Chief among them is the idea that human beings only reach their highest potential when they are actively helping others, with no thought of reward for themselves. This open orientation, Vanier argues, is the starting point on a road that will see you lose your fear of failure and grow into the truly self-actualized human being you know you can be.

There is a lesson for us at this point in the A.I.M. process from the examples of Brooks and Vanier. We began the process because there was some underlying unhappiness that was driving us to improve, to do better. While we may have begun to address that issue through the first nine stages of A.I.M., it is in this tenth and final one that we ask you to take a much bigger step. Open yourself up to helping others make their own way. Share your example with those who can learn from it. And in doing so, don't look for reward or advantage. Do it because you want to make a difference and help others to do so as well.

Moving up the A.I.M. pyramid

In his call for people to grow and orient themselves outwards, Vanier was echoing the work of psychologist Abraham Maslow. As any first-year psychology student should be able to tell you, Maslow is famous for identifying what he called a "hierarchy of needs" in human beings. His theory is that people progress upwards through a pyramid of needs. When their fundamental needs for such things as air, water, food, and shelter are met, humans can then begin to think about their safety, developing social relationships and then, self-esteem and self-confidence. When they approach the top of the pyramid, humans enter a phase Maslow called "self-actualization," where they can be creative and spontaneous, reaching their fullest potential as human beings.

While this may seem obvious to many, I have always thought there was a rough parallel in this evolution with the various levels of preparation clients have taken as I have led them through the A.I.M. process. Of the hundreds of clients I have coached over the years, I find most, at the starting point, generally fall into one of four levels on our own A.I.M. pyramid:

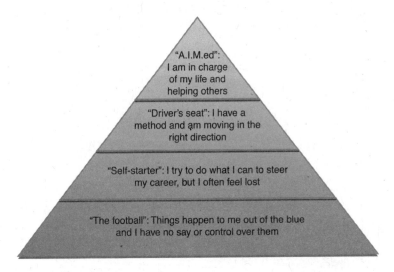

"A.I.M.ed":
I am in charge
of my life and
helping others

"Driver's seat": I have a
method and am moving in the
right direction

"Self-starter": I try to do what I can to steer
my career, but I often feel lost

"The football": Things happen to me out of the blue
and I have no say or control over them

At the bottom are individuals who have only just begun to think about making change happen for themself. They are somewhat like **footballs**, being kicked around by the whims of fate and the workplace, with little control over what is happening to them. These are the people who show up for work one day to find they have been laid off and have no idea where to turn or what to do next. These people sit at their desks every day and try to get enthused about their work, but are vaguely unhappy and haven't begun to question why. They are waiting for the next thing to happen and, when it does, wonder why it is affecting them the way it does. The bottom line with this group is, until they enter the A.I.M. process, things happen *to* them—they do not make things happen *for* themselves.

When you move up one level in the A.I.M. pyramid, you find what I call the **self-starters**. They are generally more motivated and more self-aware. They know there is something they can do to make themselves more resilient in the career world and try, with varying degrees of success, to be proactive. These are the people who look for the next course that will make them more marketable, or the project at work that might lead to a promotion. There is little method in their efforts, but they are generally aware that moving ahead takes some kind of strategic thought and are trying what they can to do something about it on their own.

As we approach the top levels of the pyramid, we find those individuals who are more or less in the **driver's seat**. They have adopted A.I.M. as a way to organize their lives and are using it to move in the right direction. While they may not have achieved the successes they set out to find just yet, they have realized that any type of life or career change requires discipline and a method to make it happen. With this in mind, they are in full flight towards achieving that goal.

At the very top of the pyramid are the people I refer to as fully **"A.I.M.ed."** These are the people who have successfully worked through the method in their initial go-round, and have adopted it as part of their regular lives. While they may not have quite achieved their life or career goals, they are generally satisfied with their level of success and the direction in which they are moving. Change for them is not something they fear, but something they embrace as a constant companion in an interesting life. They are active givers, open to helping others share in whatever wisdom or perspective their own journeys have given them.

When you spend time with people who have reached the top level of the A.I.M. pyramid, you quickly realize that there is a definite need in our society for more people with this open, giving type of orientation. All around us, we see evidence of the bonds of trust, which have made our society progressive and prosperous over the years, fraying before our eyes. With each election, the number of people who vote declines. Trust in government—and in each other—is declining as well. While crime rates have gone down, sales of security systems have gone up, driven by a *perception* that there are others, all around us, who would do us ill . Prominent examples of white-collar crime have created the perception that everyone in business is selfish, greedy, and only in it for themselves. Many issues in our society are symptomatic of such views. In my opinion, there is a simple solution: We need more people who are open, giving, and willing to help others. If more people helped others free themselves from worry and stress, then they, in turn, could give back. In short, we need more people who live the example of A.I.M. and can help others begin their journeys.

Serving as an inspirational example

Aside from helping others directly by giving them advice, we can serve as examples to inspire others to begin their own journeys or continue on the paths they have begun until they, too, begin to inspire and make a difference.

At this point in the process, you may have begun to meet people who have inspired you—people who are self-aware, open, and caring. People who are incredibly successful in their chosen endeavors, yet are still approachable and human. People who, in short, provided you with inspiration as you undertook your own journey.

We often underestimate the power of others to inspire, to give us ideas about what is possible, and how we could conduct ourselves. Yet human beings are profound followers of examples. Think about the last time you had to visit a memorial service for a friend, relative, or colleague. No matter what faith, most memorials are usually solemn affairs. People wear subdued clothing and talk in whispers. Others cry or appear sad. In general, these events are very subdued and reflective.

Now imagine if you were to take someone to a memorial service who had never attended one before. It would probably be held in a funeral home or at a house of worship that was decorated somberly, and full of people who had come to comfort the family. Within seconds of entering the room—and without you saying one word—your guest would quickly determine that this was not a place to be laughing loudly or acting foolishly. They would quickly glean from the faces and behavior of those around them how they should act. Within a few moments, they would probably be emulating what they saw around them, talking in the same hushed whispers and adapting a respectful behavior accordingly.

This is a practical example of how human beings learn how to conduct themselves from the example of others. Commentator and author Malcolm Gladwell argues that behavior that we see in others offers a guideline for how we ourselves should behave. We, in a sense, get "permission" from the environment around us about how we should act. Gladwell cites a number of instances where societies and individuals have sent messages about what is permissible and what is not. He points to the crackdown on crime in New York City in the 1990s and zero tolerance approaches to things such as subway graffiti as ways in which society set a powerful standard about what was, and was not, acceptable—a standard quickly embraced by all those who received it. On a sadder note, he highlights an epidemic of youth suicide in the Pacific Islands that was spurred by one very prominent example of a young man who took his life in response to a romance gone wrong. This event, unfortunately, gave permission to dozens of other young people to emulate the same behaviour.

A former client of mine, Rowena, found herself serving as an example to countless others without even trying. When I began coaching her, she was the vice president of a multinational medical devices company. She was balancing raising a young and growing family with her partner, along with the demands of her job. She had even found time to complete her Executive MBA. When we met, she was looking to shift from the fast-paced executive life to a position where she was more in control of her own workload and career direction. Through the A.I.M. process, she was able to identify and explore her options and, in a less than a year, had made a successful transition to setting up what would become a very successful strategic marketing consulting firm.

As she settled into her new firm, Rowena was offered a part-time teaching position at a local university. Intrigued, she began teaching business courses and quickly found she liked working with the enthusiastic young students—especially the growing number of women who were enrolling in her classes. While she was enjoying the experience immensely, she discovered, quite by accident, that her new role was having completely unintended—but positive—consequences.

After class one day, she was approached by a small group of her female students who, after some initial awkwardness about approaching their popular professor, asked her for career advice. In the discussion that followed, they confessed that they and their peers all saw her as a role model that they could only hope to emulate. As one student enthusiastically shared with her, "You have had such a great career so far, you've worked at the top ranks of a major corporation and now you have founded your own company! Do you know what learning about that does for women like us?"

The example Rowena had set had an enormous impact, and yet she was completely unconscious of it. To her, it was just who she was, but to others who may have lacked role models, she was a shining example of how women could reach the highest levels of the executive suite and still craft their life on their own terms.

Example clearly matters—so think about the example you can set for others at this point in the A.I.M. process. As someone who is in control of his or her destiny and is in a position to help others, you are on the way to becoming a person who can cause others to question their own lives and begin to move in the same positive direction. You may not realize it, but simply by sharing your experience openly and willingly, you can serve as a powerful "permission model" for others who have not yet begun their journey, or even realized that reaching this point could be possible.

Practical tips for inspiring and making a difference

Now that you are primed to begin the final two portions of the A.I.M. process—to "inspire" and "make a difference"—there are practical things you can do to make them happen. Consider the following five simple tips for putting this final stage of A.I.M. into action:

1. Don't say "no," ask "when?"

As you begin to become a potential resource and model for others, you will receive calls and e-mails at convenient, and less than convenient, times. Your phone may ring as you are running through an airport or rushing to pick the kids up from daycare. On the other end of the phone there may be someone who, much like you in your initial stages of A.I.M., is making a cold or referred call. They may be a little unsure of themselves. They may think that you have more time to talk to them than is realistically possible. They may, in short, be bothering you—and that may make you frustrated.

Our gut reaction when asked to do something that we do not have time for, or find inconvenient, is often a simple one. We say "no." Saying "no" is easy. Researchers estimate that our parents said no to us more than 100,000 times before we turned eighteen. Hundreds of times each day, we answer in the negative to an incredible range of questions and options. Our own internal voices often tell us "no" in response to the many internal conversations we have each day. As life gets busier, we are programmed for "no" as we try to retain control of our schedules.

So, when you receive that networking call from someone asking for your help, you will find yourself looking at your watch or your calendar and saying, "Gee, I'd like to meet you, but . . ." or "I don't think I am the best person to help you." In leaping to a negative response, you can always find a way to justify saying "no." "It's just this time," you might say to yourself. Or, if you are completely honest with yourself, you could find yourself thinking, "This might be a little awkward, so I don't really want to do this."

That is why, at this stage of A.I.M., your challenge is not to say "no," but to ask "when." Your task is to be open to meeting as many people as possible and to doing for them what others have done for you. Do not leap automatically to *no*; consider *when*. When can you meet with this person or give them some time on the phone? When are you able to give her or him the benefit of your experience and advice? This does not mean you have to drop everything and schedule the person in on the following day, but it does mean that you should honestly try to find time to talk with the person to help them.

"But, Jim," some people ask, "suppose I know right from the start that I can't help them?" Well, that is a good question, but let's come back to it. When you are asked to take a meeting, you have only two options: 1) do it via phone, or 2) do it in person. If, from what they are telling you in their meeting request, you really don't think you can help them as they are looking to explore an area that is outside your expertise, there is a simple way in which you can help. Schedule a brief phone call with them. Be supportive and generous with your time as you speak with them, and endeavor to think of someone in your network whom you can refer them to, once you learn more about what they are seeking to do. If your network is active and growing, you should be able to find someone who may be able to help them or connect them with others who could. In the decades I have been practicing the A.I.M. method, I have yet to find someone whom, I absolutely could not help, either with a supportive word or by connecting them with someone else in my network.

2. Share your network, don't hoard it

Human beings are naturally selfish. We often look for the possible negative outcome in any situation that involves giving up something we value in order to justify hanging on to it. In a networking situation, this can sometimes lead to what I call "hoarding" of contacts. Just as small children often clutch toys tightly to their chest and say "mine," people are often reluctant to share their network for no reason other than they do not want others to access resources they think are theirs.

Just as a child's logic about being selfish is flawed, so too is this idea that networking contacts are resources that have to be hoarded, not shared. Networking, as a practice, only works well if the network continually grows and provides benefits for everyone in it through the addition of new people. Networking is not like gold—contacts do not maintain their value if you refuse to share them. Networking contacts value their connection to you, in part, because you are helping connect them with others. Your first reaction when meeting with a new networking contact should be an open and honest feeling of "who can I connect this person with who can help them?"

This is not to say that you should immediately connect a new networking contact with every possible person in your network. One of the reasons people in your network value your referrals is that they know you will only refer others to them if you feel it is an appropriate contact. Sometimes, you will meet with people who do not make you comfortable, or who you feel may not represent you well to others. If this is the case, feel free to tell the person, "I can't think of anyone I know who would be a good contact for you," but then offer suggestions about where they might go next in following up some of the things you have discussed. Use this option rarely, however. Your default position should be an openness and willingness to help.

With such an orientation, the connections you can broker can be quite unexpected and valuable. Through the occasional coaching I do for business school graduates, I met Sayeed, a young man who was a mid-level executive in the packaging industry who was using the MBA program to explore a possible career change. While we were working through the networking stage of the A.I.M. process, he mentioned one of his former work colleagues who was now moving to a senior position with an overseas bank. As luck would have it, Sarah, another of my student coaching clients, was struggling to establish some networking contacts in the financial services industry. I asked Sayeed if he could broker a connection between Sarah and his colleague, and he quickly agreed without any hesitation. Within weeks, the two had met and found common ground. In fact, through her networking with Sayeed's colleague, Sarah was offered a position in the bank. Both of them were grateful to Sayeed for making the connection and they became the nucleus of a new part of Sayeed's network that began to reach into the financial services industry.

3. Share your own example

Most people are naturally understated. We do not generally walk down the street yelling about our accomplishments at the top of our lungs. Instead, even when we are successful, we tend to downplay our successes lest we be taken for a braggart or someone who is full of their own importance. We are even more likely to do this around others who may not be enjoying a comparable level of success, because we do not want to seem competitive or that we are belittling their contributions.

While these are good cautions, we often err too much on the side of modesty. In keeping our experiences to ourselves, we often deprive others of the example that our success could offer them. If you are truly sincere as you talk about what you are doing and how you have learned through your own experience, others will see that you are not bragging or stretching the truth.

4. Be open to serendipity

As people begin to actively network, they often put unconscious filters and barriers up when they are meeting people in their growing circle of contacts. Human beings have an unconscious predisposition to surround themselves with like-minded people—those who share similar educational backgrounds, family types, common interests, etc. This predisposition, when it creeps into networking, can often limit the breadth and depth of your potential network.

Be conscious of this predisposition. If you can keep it under control and not let it limit the scope of people you can possibly meet, you will find yourself experiencing serendipity—random good fortune—quite often with those you meet.

I recently coached Jessica, a professional magician, and recommended that others in my network meet with her as she explores her own options. However, when I have asked others to consider meeting with her, many people have raised their eyebrows, saying, "You want me to meet with a *what*?" Right away, many people doubt there would be value in meeting with someone who pulls rabbits out of hats or saws people in half. A few contacts have politely declined. But most have been open to meeting Jessica and discussing her own journey of self-discovery. By choosing to take a chance and see what happens, they have met an intelligent and very skilled young woman who takes very creative approaches to solving her problems. They have also met someone who has connected them to a broader network of people that they may never have been able to meet before—actors, artists, producers, and entertainers. By being open to the serendipity inherent in meeting many different types of people, they have broadened their networks in ways they never could have imagined.

5. Find more ways to give (and give more as you succeed)

As you move forward and become the open, networked person that you know you can be, consider the many ways that you can give back in addition to helping others through the A.I.M. process. If you do not regularly give to charities, consider doing so. Think about the issues you care about, find a few charities that deal with them, and plan your giving accordingly. Think about how you can spend your time supporting causes you care about by attending benefits, concerts, or other events that bring together like-minded people who care. If you are at a stage in your career where you can give some of your time to a cause, consider serving on the board of directors for a community organization. You will meet other people who are engaged in their community and are committed to making a difference.

As most people move forward through their careers and lives, their income increases. If this is the case for you, consider sharing your success with others by ensuring that your charitable donations increase as your income does. My co-author Alex and his wife Karen, for example, create a charitable giving plan each year when they do their taxes. This gives them a set time each year when they sit down, review how well they have done in the preceding year, and how they can share a portion of that success with others through charities they support. Other people I know follow the example set by their faith, and tithe a certain percentage of their income to good works each year. The bottom line is that success comes with the obligation to share and to help others. By doing so, you are serving as an example for others to follow. You are also opening yourself up to new experiences, new networks, and new ways to express and reinforce your giving orientation.

Henry's story: The final stages of A.I.M. throw an unexpected curve

Throughout the book, we have been relating portions of Henry's journey through the A.I.M. process. When we last touched base, he had explored his options through dozens of different meetings and had begun to build a solid network, while maintaining his commitment to his current employer as he waited to see what happened to the organization. Despite this commitment, I found Henry was becoming more and more excited about the possibilities he was uncovering through his networking. While he had planned to stay with his current employer for the short-term, I found him increasingly interested in moving on. "Jim," he said one day over coffee, "there is just so much opportunity out there that I think I may leave sooner rather than later."

Exactly one week after he made that pronouncement, fate intervened—as it often does—throwing him a curve ball. Henry and the rest of the senior management team were called into the boardroom for an unscheduled meeting with their CEO. He promptly announced that the rumored merger of the firm with a competitor was going ahead sooner than anyone could have imagined. He assured the executives that they would all have a position of some kind in the new organization. Moreover, as they all held varying stakes in the company, all members of the executive team would receive a 50 percent premium on their shares as a reward for their work with the firm, and as an incentive to stay and support the newly merged company. This generosity came with a catch, however. While members of the senior team, including Henry, stood to make a considerable amount from the takeover, the company was structuring the payments so that half would be paid once the deal was complete and the remainder would be held back for three years. If the managers left the company during that time, they would forfeit this premium. In the financial world, this is what we refer to as "golden handcuffs"— they may look good, but they trap you nonetheless.

When Henry settled into the chair opposite my desk on the day after the surprise meeting, his head was swimming. "I'm glad that they want me to stay with the company and I think there could be some good opportunities," he said, "but three years is a long time to wait. I have built up some good momentum with my networking and I don't want to put that on hold. What am I going to do now?"

Rather than tell Henry what I thought, I reverted to "coach mode" and asked him a series of questions about how he was feeling about this sudden development. Henry revealed that he was definitely of two minds about the opportunity. On the one hand, the premium he would receive on his stake in the company was a considerable sum of money—enough to make him and his family financially secure. On the other hand, he recognized that it could be a tough three years with the newly merged company. While they had guaranteed him some form of position, there was no telling where he might end up in the new structure. For all he knew, he might end up relegated to a back office in a position that was completely ill suited for him. He was also uncovering some very promising opportunities through his networking, and by putting those on hold he might be turning down something that would truly be his "dream job."

The more Henry and I talked about his decision, the more I realized that he had truly moved into the tenth and final stage of A.I.M. While this change could have a tremendous impact on him personally, most of his comments were about the impact his decision would have on others. He talked about how, by staying, he could help his colleagues weather the change. He discussed whether he would have time for his family in the hectic environment of a newly merged firm. He even talked about the example he might set for others by turning down a lucrative arrangement to pursue his own path.

I let Henry discuss his feelings for some time, and then tried to focus his thinking with one question: "Henry, if you had to pick an ideal path forward right now, what would it be?"

He paused for a moment, pursed his lips, and then chuckled. "Jim, it's probably totally unrealistic, but I'd like it if I could stay at the firm and help them get through the merger, but only if I could keep networking and exploring the world outside. It's just too much fun to not do that."

"Well, Henry," I said, "it's realistic until someone tells you not to do it. Suppose you were to pose that question to your CEO and see what he has to say?"

Henry quickly agreed, leaving my office with a bounce in his step and a new perspective on his new work situation. The next morning, he met with his CEO over coffee, and sketched out his situation. As Henry later told me, he explained simply that he was excited about what was happening and then asked a basic question: "What can I do to help you make this happen?"

Henry found that his CEO was incredibly open to his honesty and his offer to help. In the conversation that followed, his CEO outlined the sheer number of details that the company now had to manage with respect to the merger. They were confident of the value that the newly merged company could provide in the market, but they were facing an overwhelming avalanche of details that the team would have to wade through before the deal could be finalized. Issues such as bringing two staff cultures together, amalgamating locations and offices, securing bridge financing for the venture, communicating with customers and suppliers—the list was long and complex, and it was clear to Henry that his superior was finding it stressful. "Henry, this merger will be good, but few of us have been through this before," he confided. "It's too bad we don't have someone in either company who has."

"Well," Henry replied, "I haven't been through a merger, but I do know someone who should be able to help."

If you recall from our previous chapter, in the course of his networking efforts Henry had met with Joel, the head of a venture capital firm who had helped him understand the world of financing, mergers, and acquisitions. His advice to Henry had been to gain a few more years of experience before exploring the world of investment firms, advice that Henry had taken to heart. He had kept in touch with Joel as his network continued to grow, and now, Henry was in the unique position of being able to offer to connect his CEO with Joel—someone who could help him with the upcoming merger. A quick e-mail from Henry brought Joel into the loop, and a few days later, both of them were having an animated breakfast conversation with Henry's CEO to discuss some of the issues the company was facing.

In the next few weeks, things moved fairly quickly. Joel's firm was retained to advise Henry's company on the financial aspects of the merger. More importantly, the CEO asked Henry to take responsibility for liaising with Joel, and gave him responsibility for several of the key stakeholder issues. In asking Henry to shepherd supplier and client relations over the merger period, he specifically singled out his growing external network and ability to broker new relationships as the reason behind his choice. "We need someone who can keep a lot of people happy and in the tent, Henry," he explained. "And from what I've seen, that's you."

Henry was a little dazed as he explained this turn of events to me. "Jim, I could never have done this just a few years ago, and now look where I have ended up." With this appointment, Henry now had a respected position in his firm that essentially gave him the opportunity to continue to enhance his network while learning more about the broader business world. Moreover, the next three years leading up to his payout would be challenging and full of personal and professional growth.

When I last touched base with Henry, he was thriving in his new position. The merger had gone more smoothly than people had expected. He had also taken on a new and unexpected role in the newly merged company. A younger generation of leadership was moving up the ranks of the firm and now looked to him as a mentor. In addition to his external network, he was actively coaching several protégés within the firm, connecting them with others in his network and advising them on their professional and personal challenges. One of his new colleagues had told him in an unguarded moment that others in the firm saw him as a model of what an executive could be. "You're out there representing the company, you are on top of your game, yet you always have time for people like us," he had said. "You have no idea how much we respect that."

Henry shared that story with me with some amusement, and then went on to add that he and his wife were already thinking about what they could do with the delayed bonus when the three years were up. "We know we will probably travel and put some aside for retirement," Henry confided, "but we're also thinking about setting up a foundation to promote education. We haven't thought through the details yet, but we both decided that some of this should go back to where it can do some good for people we don't even know yet."

Rarely in my coaching career have I seen such a complete—and rewarding—transformation. From a person who was unhappy and unsure of what he wanted to do, Henry had grown through the various A.I.M. stages into a confident executive who was in control of his life and loving his work. His open and engaging orientation, and the network he had developed because of it, had not gone unnoticed by either his CEO or his colleagues. He now found himself becoming not only a leader within the executive team, but also a role model for other employees across the organization. And to top it off, his financial position had improved to the extent that he and his wife could now think about what they could do to give back to the community.

"Part of me wants to say I've been lucky, Jim," he confided to me, "but I know that the method helped prepare me for the opportunity that came along. Without that, I would never have been able to even think about what I am doing now."

Our journey together is over, but yours continues

With the close of this chapter, our journey together through the A.I.M. process also comes to a close. We began at a starting point of uncertainty and questioning, but began to move forward. We have progressed through a series of exercises that have helped you to get to know yourself better, moving on to others that have helped you begin to identify what you want to do and—more importantly—how to achieve it. You've been shown how to prioritize your options and conduct research with respect to them. Through the networking portions of the process, you have begun to build the most important resource to help you explore and realize your new directions—a broad network of people who can connect you with others and provide you with opportunities and information.

Finally, in this chapter, we have explained the ultimate conclusion of A.I.M.—to allow you to inspire others and make a difference not only with respect to yourself, but also those around you. If you have successfully completed the A.I.M. process, you are now a rarity among others—someone who has identified what they want to do with a method to achieve it. Through this process, you have left the ranks of those who want to make change happen but can't quite figure out how, and have now become one of those few individuals who can make change happen for themselves. You can now help make change happen for others. As you move forward, take your duty of serving as an inspirational example and as a coach and confidant to heart. By helping others change as you yourself have changed, the world can change in turn.

As we close this book, consider the following words from the German thinker Goethe: *Whatever you can do or dream you can, begin it. Boldness has genius, power, and magic in it.*

Be bold. Be thoughtful. Be thorough. And A.I.M. high.

PART III

Wrapping Up and Looking Forward

A.I.M. in a Shifting Market

It is confidence in our bodies, minds, and spirits that allows us to keep looking for new adventures, new directions to grow in, and new lessons to learn— which is what life is all about.

—Oprah Winfrey

As Alex and I finish our work on this book, the world economy is still very much in flux. Some markets are still experiencing high levels of unemployment, growing uncertainty, downsizing in the workplace, and rising feelings of despair and hopelessness. Others are beginning to show some initial signs of recovery, but many of these signs are tenuous and have yet to take root to the extent that they can overcome the fear and wariness that began to sweep across the world in 2008.

Such an uncertain economy would seem like an unlikely place for a new beginning for your career and life. But that is exactly what dozens of my coaching clients have found over the years. I have lived and worked through several major and minor recessions. During all of them, the A.I.M. method has helped people focus, overcome their challenges, and move their lives forward.

My work with Mike in the recession that followed the horrors of the 9/11 attacks offers a good example. He was a graduate of a business school at one of the major universities I work with. One day when I was on campus coaching some MBA students, a professor approached me to ask me for a favor for a former student of his.

He explained that Mike had been an exemplary student in the school's Executive MBA program just a few years earlier. The program took a grueling two years to complete and saw professionals devote thirty hours per week to their studies, over and above their demanding day jobs. Mike, the professor explained, had passed through the program with flying colors, but was now facing some significant challenges.

I invited Mike to my home for our initial chat. On the surface, he was upbeat and pleasant, discussing his career and professional interests. His expertise was in marketing, but he was well versed in IT. His previous employer, an international retail company, had earmarked him as a high-potential senior manager and paid for his MBA. I could see, however, that Mike's story was a good front that masked some serious worries on his part.

After he had completed his MBA, Mike explained, things began to go badly for him. The executive who had encouraged him to do his MBA had left the company suddenly. His new manager didn't necessarily see value in the MBA the company had paid for—or in Mike for that matter. After some awkwardness and some uncertain performance feedback, Mike decided to move on, joining an entrepreneurial IT company that appeared to have a strong future. Unfortunately, he joined just in time for the dot-com implosion and the downturn that followed 9/11.

By the time Mike met me, he had been out of work for a year, pounding the pavement between meetings and interviews. He was running short of money and was wondering how he could contribute his share to his family's mortgage payments and support his two growing boys. On the verge of personal bankruptcy, he was working in a lumberyard just to get by.

In many ways, he was already practicing many of the components of the A.I.M. method. He was an articulate networker who had packaged himself well. But for whatever reason, his efforts were not paying off. And that presented me with a challenge—what more could I do to help this guy?

After I had heard Mike's story, I realized that the last thing he needed was another person to feel sorry and empathize with him. Instead, I reviewed every component of his search strategy with him, asking critical questions about what he had, and hadn't, done. It quickly became apparent that he was lacking in two key areas of the A.I.M. method. His networking approach definitely needed work, and his toolkit could use some serious improvement.

With respect to networking, he had been active, but had confined himself to a narrow segment of potential contacts, which he had almost exhausted. It was clear to me that he needed to refresh his efforts and refocus on other markets related to the options he had identified. I was happy to provide him with some additional research suggestions and even offered some initial contacts from my own network that he could explore, which he pursued eagerly and productively.

With respect to his toolkit, Mike faced some definite challenges. While he was articulate, he had not yet figured out how to position his story to interest those in his network or potential employers. He came across as a little confused and unfocused when he talked about his experience and the possible contribution he could make to a new workplace. We worked on improving his elevator speech about himself, his needs, and what he had to offer others. We also focused on the ways he could approach future networking meetings in terms of their purpose and his expectations.

After several months of hard work on these and other fronts, Mike had a breakthrough. He landed a contract position back in the retail business and, while impressing his new employer, used it to continue expanding his network and investigating his opportunities through the A.I.M. method. With this change of fortune, he was pumped, gave great value to his employer, and became quite an expert in the marketing/technology field. As the end of his contract approached, he new the odds weren't great that it would be extended. Re-energized, he hit the ground running and ramped up his networking even further. From his growing network of contacts, Mike was able to land another contract position that, in turn, led to a full-time position in the field. Within several months of addressing his issues and renewing his networking, Mike was able to get his career—and his life—back on track.

Today, many years later, Mike is an A.I.M. success story. Master of his own fate, he is in a senior consulting role with an international technology company, working from his family's new home in the country. Mike has also turned into a bit of an apostle of the A.I.M. method, and is helping others deal with the same types of circumstances in which he found himself.

So what worked for Mike? His persistence, diligence, and openness to outside advice were a perfect match for the rigorous method of A.I.M. Together, these factors helped him address a major challenge that could have kept others stalled in the lumberyard. Today, Mike continues to practice A.I.M. principles and knows that if another downturn comes, he is better prepared than ever to move forward and remain the "boss" of his career.

As Mike's journey from the lumberyard back to the top ranks of his career shows, downturns can be opportunities. There are also opportunities if you find yourself starting the A.I.M. process when others would say you are on top of your game. I've had numerous clients who needed a process to move ahead, despite appearing to an outside observer to be focused, achieving their dreams, and benefiting from an upswing in their segment of the economy.

As the financial crisis began to take hold across the world in 2008, I began coaching Samir, a young executive in his early thirties who, at first glance, didn't seem to need the help that I could provide.

Samir came to me upon the recommendation of a colleague of his who had worked with me previously. We met at my home office and, as we settled into the easy chairs over a coffee, I took stock of what appeared to be a very self-assured person. He had greeted me warmly and, in response to my question "tell me about yourself," had told a very straightforward and well-organized story. After graduating with his MBA several years ago, he had begun working for an insurance company and had risen to a senior position in the financial services department. Married with a small child, he and his wife were looking forward to building a good life together in the coming years, as he hit his stride as a professional.

As he spoke, I was already feeling challenged and wondered what value I could potentially provide to Samir. In an economy that was moving sideways, he had a good job and seemed to be focused and comfortable enough to move forward in his career. In short, he seemed to have everything under control—so why had he been referred to me?

When Samir began discussing where he wanted to move in his career path, however, the picture became a little more cloudy.

"I've already identified several possible options I'd like to explore, Jim, I just need to get moving—so I'd like some advice." He then shared a list of possible new career options, all of which were in the alternative energy field. As we talked, Samir told me he was concerned that the insurance company was not dynamic enough for him, and that he was very interested in all the attention that was being focused on newer, environmental firms. He clearly became excited and engaged as he talked about the opportunities in this field, and the long-term nature of the type of business leadership that would be required to help society deal with its environmental challenges.

"I am really interested in this field," he added. "I just need a strategy to explore my options further."

While I was impressed with Samir's passion for this new career options, his idea of making a foray into a new market during a recession raised a few red flags for me. Potential employers and networking contacts might think, "Wait a minute—you have a great life now and you want to rush off and try something new in the worst job market in a generation?" If they did respond that way, they might not see Samir as a serious professional—or worse, see him as someone who took his current opportunities for granted. I was also concerned that he had assumed that he would be a fine fit for the alternative energy field, without having first checked on whether he was qualified and would be taken seriously.

I broached both concerns with him, frankly advising that, unless he dealt with these concerns, his networking strategy might fail just as he came out of the gate. "Aren't you concerned," I asked, "that if you can't explain why you want to move on, others might think you are taking a good position for granted? Don't you think that some firms might think, 'Wait, he's an insurance guy. What does he know about alternative energy?'"

Samir gave me a funny look, but then the light began to dawn on his face. "I never thought of it that way, Jim," he replied. "I've been thinking about this from my viewpoint so far, and haven't thought what others might think. I'm not in a hurry—so let's do this right." We rolled up our sleeves and got to work.

Our first task was to work on his elevator speech to address questions around why he wanted to explore options beyond his current career and why he was interested in alternative energy. With this in hand, we then moved on to his research and networking strategy. I quickly determined that he was looking at *all* the companies that were in the alternative energy market. With such a breadth of possible areas to explore, this made any effective strategy almost impossible to succeed. Through some questions and further research, we were able to identify a subset of alternative energy firms that he could explore as a starting point. We then moved on to his networking strategy. Samir already had some networks in place and had made some initial contacts, but had not conducted thorough research or mapped out his course of action. Through our discussion, we identified some sources in the industry he might want to explore, such as associations, universities, and venture capital firms.

With this strategy—and a good elevator speech—in place, Samir was now ready to move on to explore his options properly. As he began meeting with networking contacts, he found many were very sensitive about the uncertain nature of the current job market. In these cases, he found that the work he had done to tailor his message to this market paid off handsomely. Within a few weeks, he realized that he had a lot to learn about the environmental business world. He redoubled his networking efforts and began serving on the board of a non-governmental organization (NGO) working in his area to pick up some more practical intelligence and experience in the area.

While Samir's journey remained a work in progress at the time of writing, it does illustrate that even outwardly successful people who are secure in a shifting market can find value in the A.I.M. method—particularly its emphasis on how your search will be perceived by those you contact.

As you consider your own position in the world that is emerging from a recession, think of Mike and Samir. In one case, a professional was broadsided by an economic downturn and found himself working in a lumberyard to make ends meet while he got back on his feet. In the other, a professional with everything going for him still needed a method, and some advice, to explore his options during a recession. In each case, A.I.M. gave them a method to follow as they assessed what they wanted and then moved forward—and it can be just as useful to you, no matter where you find yourself in this uncertain economy.

Further Reading Recommendations

There are literally thousands of books you can read about self-improvement, coaching, or identifying what you want to do in life. The books listed below offer a different perspective, asking you to step outside many of the books that are often circular, self-serving and, at the end of the day, tell you things you already know.

These four books (two of which we mentioned in this book) will give you that different perspective on why people give, the roles people play in society, and how individuals can truly make a difference:

Arthur C. Brooks. *Who Really Cares*. New York: Basic Books, 2006.
This is a good book about who gives to charity in the United States and why. If you want to learn more about how your own giving behavior may be influenced by your upbringing, religious/secular orientation, or other factors, this book works well to provide an interesting perspective that has attracted criticism and praise from different commentators.

Bill Cohen. *Life Mapping.* **New York: Harper Collins, 1998.**
Cohen's book outlines how you can explore the "four dimensions" of your personality that A.I.M. uses as the basis of the windowpane exercise. As we point out, people often ignore the other dimensions of their lives in favor of focusing exclusively on their professional achievements— something that Cohen's book does an excellent job of explaining.

Malcolm Gladwell. *The Tipping Point: How Little Things Can Make a Big Difference.* **New York: Little Brown and Company, 2000.**
Gladwell bills this book as one that is about "how little things make a big difference." Aside from the points we noted in A.I.M. (such as his observations about permission models and the role of connectors), his book offers an engagingly written examination of how he thinks things in society really work.

Greg Mortenson and David Oliver Relin. *Three Cups of Tea: One Man's Mission to Promote Peace . . . One School at a Time.* **New York: Viking Press, 2006.**
If ever you doubt that one individual can overcome significant obstacles and have an unimaginable impact on the world, read this book. Greg Mortensen was a mountain climber who, while working as a nurse, was living out of his car. A change of direction while climbing Pakistan's K2 saw him begin building schools for deprived communities in the high Himalayas. Now, decades later, reading about the impact that basic education is having on these communities is truly inspiring.

About the Authors

Jim Carlisle

Jim Carlisle is an internationally recognized management coach and consultant, specializing in executive search. The A.I.M. method grew from his more than 30 years of experience working with hundreds of clients who have ranged from top executives to recent MBA graduates.

Jim began his career with Bank of Montreal in the late 1960s and branched into the world of management consulting several years later. He specialized in executive search, first with The Caldwell Partners and then as a partner with Ernst and Young. Jim decided he'd like to build his own firm and currently is a Director of Western Management Consultants, where he focuses on executive search and coaching. He also serves as chair of the World Search Alliance and travels regularly to many countries to work with top executives.

Jim has been married to his wife Lynne, a communications professional and educator, for more than 40 years. They reside in Oakville, Ontario.

Alex Gill

Alex Gill is a social entrepreneur who enjoys working with community activists, nonprofit executives and others who want to make a difference. He currently heads Mendicant Group, a consultancy that helps charities and nonprofit organizations improve their social impact. Prior to founding Mendicant, Alex spent more than a dozen years as an executive at a number of large nonprofits. Mendicant's clients include a diverse range of NGOs, including those working in such areas as health care, child and youth development, and the environment.

In addition to his community focus, Alex teaches at Toronto's Ryerson University in the Department of Politics and Public Administration. Each year, he introduces hundreds of students to the fields of corporate citizenship, advocacy and social marketing.

Alex and his wife Karen spend as much time during the summer as they can on the Bay of Exploits on the northeast coast of Newfoundland. For the remainder of the year, they live and work in downtown Toronto.

Index

Following this subject index is an index of case studies of clients of the A.I.M. program.

Pages in **bold face** indicate pages with diagrams or graphs.

Index of Case Studies

Preceding this case studies index is a general subject index.

Pages in **bold face** indicate pages with diagrams or graphs.